I Chose Adventism

I Chose Adventism

William and Noelene Johnsson

Review and Herald Publishing Association
Washington, DC 20039-0555
Hagerstown, MD 21740

The authors assume full responsibility for the accuracy of all facts and quotations as cited in this book.

This book was
Edited by Richard W. Coffen
Designed by Dennis Ferree
Cover Design by Bryan Gray
Cover Photos by Dave Sherwin, Tom Radcliffe, Meylan Thoresen, and Charles Whieldon.
Type set: 11/12 Sabon

PRINTED IN U.S.A.

Library of Congress Cataloging in Publication Data

Johnsson, William G., 1934–
I chose Adventism/William and Noelene Johnsson.
p. cm.

1. Seventh-day Adventists—Doctrines. 2. Adventists—Doctrines.
3. Johnsson, William G., 1934- I. Johnsson, Noelene, 1938-
II. Title.
BX6154.J64 1988
248.4'86732—dc19 87-25370
CIP

ISBN 0-8280-0407-2

Dedicated to
Fred Taylor and Joel Johnsson—
our fathers
who first chose

CONTENTS

PREFACE

We have written this book for people who have chosen Adventism or who are contemplating doing so.

If we take Adventism seriously—and we should—it impacts all of life. Adventists hold a common faith, share a common hope, seek to complete a common mission, and follow a common lifestyle. More than most religions, Adventism is a way of life.

I (William) have been an Adventist for many years, but I wasn't always one. After I joined the church, almost daily I faced a series of new and sometimes troubling questions. An invitation to a party—should I accept? A forthcoming wedding—could I feel free to attend? Work or travel possibilities—would they compromise my earnestness in keeping the Sabbath?

I tended to be very cautious. Usually it seemed easier to say no than to run the risk of new situations where my newfound faith, so precious to me, might be imperiled.

I was probably too cautious. I probably said no to invitations and possibilities that the Lord had placed before me. I wish that I had found someone who could have given me a perspective on the way in which Adventists—especially new ones—might relate to relatives, friends, and work and social situations.

Hence this book. I have been a student among non-Adventists. I have worked in a non-Adventist environment. I have friends and many relatives who do not share my religious convictions. This book is a distillation of my own experiences and observations, augmented by the discussions and conversations with others that my wife, Noelene, and I have had. And without exception, the people with whom we talked wished that after they had joined the church they had related more positively to relatives and friends.

Noelene and I hope that Adventists who have grown up in the church will also find the book useful. Regardless of whether we have just joined the church or whether our Adventism dates back four generations, we face a common question: How does the Lord want us to live in the world? If we say yes to people and possibilities, will we gradually compromise our faith? If we say no to them, do we settle for a restricted, even shriveled, existence that denies the fullness of life the Lord wants us to show to the world?

I've never regretted my decision to become an Adventist. Through this people the Lord has nourished and sustained me. He has given me a place to belong and joys more abundant every day.

We hope that will be your experience also, and that this book will help you find it.

1

My Path to Adventism

I made the decision for Adventism carefully, after much thought and in the face of family pressures and other options.

My father had belonged to the Adventist Church for many years. Born in Stockholm, Sweden, into a Lutheran home, by age 16 he went to sea. He sailed the world, first on sailing ships and later on steam vessels. Twice he sailed around Cape Horn, before the Panama Canal was finished. He used to tell us children stories of being months at sea without seeing land, of unscrupulous captains and ship's pursers who bought substandard food for the sailors and pocketed the rest of the funds, of a sick sailor put ashore and left to die alone in a strange land.

One day Father's ship sailed into Port Adelaide in South Australia. Whatever the reason (I never did find out), when his ship sailed on, Father was not on board. He settled in South Australia, for several years sailing on boats around the Australian seaports.

One evening he sat in the sailors' hall, listening to a concert put on by a glee club. The singers had come from an Anglican church in Adelaide, but his gaze stayed on only one person in the choir, a pretty young woman with dark hair and strong, bright eyes.

They met and felt attracted to each other. His English was poor and thickly accented. She came from a line of proper

Anglicans who dated back to the first settlers in the colony, staunch churchgoers, choir members at St. Andrew's church, respected in the town.

They fell in love and planned marriage. Her family wasn't happy—this wasn't the scenario her parents had planned. But she knew what she wanted. She would trust her heart against their misgivings. And he was a good man, true and straightforward despite his foreign accent.

So Edith Painter married Joel Johnsson in St. Andrew's.

A child was born. Then another. Joel quit sailing and found work as a smelter, melting down ingots from lead ore. Later he became a builder. He was big, strong, and healthy and brought home good pay. The crash of 1929 was still 10 years away.

But one Sunday afternoon something happened that would change the direction of Joel's life. With time on his hands, he went to the city park, where on a given Sunday anyone could set up a soapbox and set the world straight about politics, economics, or philosophy—

Or religion.

As Joel wandered among atheists, political candidates, and snake-oil healers haranguing languid listeners, he came upon a quiet, dignified man telling about Bible prophecies. Joel paused to listen—and that was the first stage in his path to Adventism.

Many years later I used to hear Father say, "Believe your beliefs and doubt your doubts." He was telling us to think our convictions through carefully—and then to stay with them all the way.

That was the pattern of his life. Unswerving in his devotion to the Lord, he became Adventist to the roots of his being.

Edith agreed to study her husband's newfound faith. But something went wrong. She was put off by the minister's insensitivity. He wanted to sit down and teach Bible doctrines to her even though her babies were crying and needed attention. Her religion was staunchly practical—even into her old age. She would bring lonely people home from nursing homes and provide them a Christmas dinner—and she decided that no matter how right the minister might be in his ideas, his example did not measure up.

Mother never did choose Adventism. Although she completed housecleaning on Friday and prepared Sabbath meals before sunset, although she accompanied Father to church and in later years came out to hear me preach, she remained an Anglican to the day of her death.

So the Johnsson home had parents who were God-fearing but divided in their choice of denomination. Father was a Seventh-day Adventist, Mother an Anglican. And I, youngest of the nine, to this day am the only child to choose Adventism.

Ours was a vigorous, freethinking family. I see it yet—the long table with all of us seated around it, Father at the head and Mother opposite him, constantly bobbing up and down to bring food from the stove. We discussed and argued about religion, politics, football, cricket. Usually several people would be speaking at once.

When I was growing up, we must have been poor—I was born in the depths of the Great Depression—but at the time that thought never entered my mind. Instead of thinking about how poor we were, the family thought about *work*. Father and Mother always seemed to be working. When the building industry failed, Father started his own small business. Mother cooked, cleaned, sewed, washed, ironed, and darned long after we fell asleep. I remember the copper laundry vessel in which she boiled the clothes, the corrugated scrubbing board, the old wood stove.

Out of this social and religious mix, I chose Adventism. Why, when my eight older siblings did not? Only the Lord knows the whole story, but I think of two factors.

First, my father lived his religion. My first memory of him is the same as the last—early in the morning, seated alone in the quietness of the living room, studying his Bible. Although he had little formal education, he had great wisdom. For years he immersed himself in the study of the Bible until he knew it like no other person I've met. For many years he taught a Sabbath school class, always on time Sabbath morning to meet his students until his 80th year, when he entered the hospital for his last illness.

Father served for years as a member of the conference executive committee. He became acquainted with leaders of the church in the South Pacific and occasionally with some from the General Conference. Though he would have known something of the frailty of leaders and the mistakes that sometimes accompany the work of the church, the spirit he conveyed was one of loyalty and devotion to the cause.

He transmitted that to me.

The second factor that no doubt influenced me to choose Adventism was Adventist literature.

Several of my older brothers and sisters had the opportunity of attending Seventh-day Adventist elementary schools, which I never did. However, Father made sure that I was exposed to Adventist publications. He didn't demand that I read this or that, he didn't command or require. He simply left copies of *Signs of the Times,* the *Australasian Record, Steps to Christ, The Desire of Ages,* and the Sabbath school lesson quarterly around the house. Occasionally I would see issues of the *Review and Herald,* known today as the *Adventist Review,* from the United States. He encouraged me to read the Bible, to form the habit of daily study, and to search its truths for myself.

I was an avid reader. I read the Adventist literature he left around, and I read myself into Adventism. As a teenager, I gradually became more interested in *Steps to Christ, The Desire of Ages,* and *Daniel and Revelation* than in playing on my school's football team on Saturdays.

One day I accepted my father's invitation to go with him to church. I began to attend regularly. Then came an evangelistic effort held in the Adelaide town hall by George Burnside. I sat through the meetings and went down into the baptismal tank the same night the preacher spoke on the topic of baptism.

It wasn't an easy decision. I didn't make it quickly—it was several years in forming. My brothers and sisters, most of whom were still living at home, were watching.

Sensing what was happening, one of them invited me to go for a ride on his motorcycle one evening. After we had sped over the miles, with the wind licking our faces, he stopped at a dairy bar. Over milk shakes, he said, "I've been noticing a change in you. You seem to be getting pretty interested in going to church with Dad. That's all right. But don't do anything yet—wait until you're at least 18. Then you'll know if you really want to be a Seventh-day Adventist."

But I had already joined the baptismal class. I had heard the call of Jesus. He had spoken to my heart, and I had said yes. I've never regretted it.

The hardest part was in relating to my mother. I was her youngest and had been born fairly late in her life. She looked upon me as something of a miracle child. We were very close. In choosing Adventism, was I in some sense repudiating what she stood for?

But Mother and I grew together as a result of my choice. We both learned that in choosing Adventism, I did not and would not love her less.

I love the Lord. I love His people. The decision I made as a 15-year-old boy growing up in southern Australia changed my life. It set me on a course that I could not have dreamed of at that time. That one day I would follow the Lord's further calling and become a minister, that I would sail away from my homeland and with my wife serve as a missionary in India, that eventually we would make the United States our adopted home—who could have imagined the future?

Of all the many decisions I have made over the years, that

one—the decision to choose Adventism—undoubtedly was the most important of my life.

Yet for all the joy and fulfillment it has brought me, it was not without pain. Relatives, friends, work, play—I faced the tricky task of relating to each. And that is why I write this book.

Noelene grew up in an Adventist home. A minister's daughter, she learned early what it means to belong to the "Advent movement," as old-timers refer to the church. The family had lived in five widely separated towns and cities of Australia and New Zealand by the time she was 13.

But even though you are brought up to love the Lord and accept the Adventist lifestyle, there comes a time when you must decide for yourself whether or not to follow the religion of your parents. "At age 12 I wanted to be baptized," she says. "But by the time I turned 13, I had changed my mind. I rebelled at having to be so different from everybody else."

What probably made the biggest difference in helping her choose Adventism was getting back into an Adventist school when the family moved from Invercargill, New Zealand, to Melbourne, Australia. There was no getting away from God's love. She had to face up to it and make a decision. "And ever since, I have feared anything that might tempt me to go back on my choice, to give up my faith."

Children were brought up quite strictly in the faith back in the thirties and forties. Sabbath was more likely to be a long day of don'ts than it is today. Punishments for infractions of the rules were swift and sure. Consequently, the incidence of rebellious children was probably higher than it is today. Today's young Adventists typically decide to join the church at around age 12. For some, a testing of their beliefs comes later in the teens, but for many, possibly most, the real testing comes after graduation from college. Young people at some point must face the question: Am I in this because I am following my parents, or because I choose it for myself. The later the question is faced, the more traumatic the decision is likely to be.

"I chose Adventism," Noelene says. "My roots have grown ever deeper in the soil in which I was nourished. I feel a real loyalty to the church and to my Saviour. I have found fulfillment by joining God's people."

Others Who Chose Adventism

On average, more than 1,000 people join the SDA Church every day. Their paths to Adventism are as varied as life. Here are a few vignettes:

Samson Kisekka, prime minister of Uganda, and a physician, became an Adventist as the result of a chance visit to an evangelistic meeting. Later Earl E. Cleveland's meetings grounded him in the faith. Dr. Kisekka owned a hospital, a farm, and other industries. He organized Adventist laypeople into an association that would help disadvantaged people make an effort to help themselves.

When Idi Amin came to power in Uganda and banned the Seventh-day Adventist Church, Dr. Kisekka's foundation sustained our people. In the turmoil that followed Amin's ouster, Dr. Kisekka had to flee for his life. His home was burned and his property looted. But at last his countrymen turned to him, calling him from exile in 1986 to be prime minister of the war-ravaged land. They looked for a man of integrity to help restore stability and order.

Michele Bush, crack sprinter at UCLA, established NCAA track records. She refuses to compete on Sabbaths. In 1984 she forfeited a possible berth on the U.S. Olympic squad when she refused to compete on Sabbath for the Olympic tryouts. She chose Adventism over fame.

Herbert Blomstedt conducts the San Francisco Symphony Orchestra. Swedish born son of an Adventist minister, Dr. Blomstedt is internationally acclaimed for the precision and sensitivity of his interpretation. In musical circles he is also known for his vegetarian lifestyle and adherence to Sabbathkeeping. Although Blomstedt conducts certain classical music during the Sabbath, all his contracts state that he will not be required to rehearse with the orchestra from Friday sunset to Saturday sunset.

Herbert Doggette, Jr., is the deputy commissioner of operations for the United States Social Security Administration. As number two person in the huge department, Doggette oversees the work of 65,000 employees and handles $200 billion in benefit payments and a $2 billion administrative budget. He has succeeded in government because of his faithfulness to duty and his passion for excellence in everything he does. A loyal Adventist, Doggette has held almost every office in his local church.

Clarence Hodges is deputy assistant secretary for the United States Department of State. In the pursuit of U.S. foreign policy, he travels worldwide, meets world leaders, and faces dangerous high-pressure situations. Nevertheless, he maintains an active church life as a committed Seventh-day Adventist.

Raoul Dederen, professor of systematic theology and associate dean of the SDA Theological Seminary, grew up a Roman Catholic in Belgium. His parents had mapped out a bright future for him in the diplomatic corps of his country. But in the midst of his studies he chose Adventism as the result of meeting some SDA young people on a toboggan run. His father, a textile factory manager, strongly opposed Raoul's decision. At the conclusion of a long conversation that failed to dissuade Raoul, he said, "I pray to God that He will spare you the experience of having a son come to you one day to ask your permission to become a monk!"

Joseph Bates, retired sea captain, gave all that he had to proclaim the message of the soon coming of Jesus and of the seventh day Sabbath. He became one of the pioneer leaders of the fledgling Seventh-day Adventist Church.

James White poured his considerable energies into the young Adventist movement. The founder and first editor of the *Review and Herald,* James traveled, wrote, preached, and organized, helping to transform Seventh-day Adventism into an established church.

Ellen Harmon, later the wife of James White, became Adventism's most prominent person. Like James White and Joseph Bates, she chose to follow the teachings of the Bible rather than the beliefs of the popular churches. She threw in her lot with the Adventists while still a teenager.

Although she was shy and had little formal education, the Lord used her to bring messages to His people. While only 17 she received a vision—the first of hundreds from the Lord, given during a ministry that spanned nearly 70 years. She became the church's most prolific writer. Her messages of comfort, rebuke, and counsel continue to guide Adventism.

Saul of Tarsus, persecutor of Christians, met Jesus as he journeyed on the road to Damascus. In blinding light he chose Jesus as Saviour and Lord. Jesus chose him to spread Christianity among the Gentiles. Preacher and writer of the Second Coming, apostle of the early church, Saul/Paul practiced the keeping of the seventh-day Sabbath.

Paul may have been married when he accepted Jesus. If so, his marriage did not survive his conversion: Paul conducted his ministry as a single person. The New Testament gives only one reference to his relatives—a nephew (Acts 23:16). When Paul declared his loss of all things for Christ (Philippians 3:8), he probably included family and former friends.

And Jesus Himself kept the Sabbath (Luke 4:16). Although denominations did not exist when He was on earth—He is the way, the truth, and the life for all Christians—we look upon Him as the first "Seventh-day Adventist" in the Christian era, because He promised, "I will come again, and receive you unto myself" (John 14:3).

Jesus committed Himself to the Father's will. He chose the life—and death—that would bring us salvation. His brothers and sisters, older than He, did not understand or appreciate His mission. Even His mother pondered the ways of her remarkable son. He died at 33, a single, but His mission was completed.

His choice for us all makes possible our choice for Him.

2

When Your Spouse Doesn't Choose Adventism

Noelene and I are both Seventh-day Adventists. We became acquainted at Avondale College in Australia—an Adventist institution—and as the attraction deepened, above all else we desired to worship together on Friday evenings and Sabbath mornings.

But suppose your spouse has not chosen to be an Adventist? Suppose your spouse once belonged to the Adventist Church, but for whatever reason severed those ties? How will you relate to him or her? Will you find yourselves going different ways? Should you demand that your spouse choose Adventism, which to you is clearly the most important thing in the world? How can you go on living with your spouse without compromising your faith?

Here's how Clara handled the situation.

When Clara married Ken, neither was a practicing Christian. Ken had been raised a Roman Catholic, Clara a Protestant; but both had long since ceased attending church. They found a Protestant minister to marry them, and for many years they lived together reasonably happy. They had three children.

But as the children grew up and left home, the marriage began to disintegrate. Ken, always a drinker, began spending too many evenings at the local sports club, joining his male friends in drinking bouts. More and more his chain-smoking irritated Clara, who does not smoke. She had not worked outside the home after marriage—Ken seemed threatened by that option—so felt hemmed in by her marriage. As they grew further apart, she felt as though the walls of her life were closing around her.

One day a neighbor invited Clara to attend church with her. Clara accepted. She began to attend church on a regular basis and for the first time in her life she experienced the reality of Jesus as Saviour and Lord. Suddenly life came together with a dimension she had never experienced before: she found peace, joy, and fulfillment.

But Ken had no interest in religion. The door of the church made him feel uncomfortable. He almost had to be dragged inside for a wedding or a funeral. He looked with amusement, then skepticism, finally resignation, on Clara's newfound faith.

At first Clara hoped that Ken would want to share the new life which meant so much to her. She prayed and watched for evidences of his turning to the Lord. But they didn't come, and she grew disappointed and frustrated. Now his heavy drinking disgusted her, and she wished she could live in a home free of tobacco smoke.

Clara began to think of leaving Ken. The children had left the nest; so would she. After all, for years they had had no real communication. They had been going separate ways, and Clara's decision to follow Jesus had simply widened the gap.

But first she sounded out a Christian counselor. He encouraged her not to break up the marriage, but to face Ken squarely with the situation, to tell him just how she felt and thereby to find a way to save the marriage.

Clara did so. At first Ken didn't want to talk about it at all. He provided a home and food for her, he said. Wasn't that enough? "No," said Clara, "it isn't enough." Unless they could come to a clear understanding, unless they could find a closeness in their marriage, what was the point of living together?

Finally Ken and Clara worked their way through to an understanding. Past the anger. Past the hurt feelings. Past the unfulfilled expectations. Past the misunderstandings. Past the pettiness. Past the meanness toward each other.

Yes, Ken would spend more time with Clara, less with "the boys." He would try to drink less. He wouldn't go to church with her, but she could practice her religion any way she pleased. And yes—it took a great effort—she was free to look for a job, provided it didn't mean that he had to prepare the meals or do the housework.

For more than five years now Ken and Clara have had a reasonably good marriage. Though Clara hates having to go to church on her own, though she wishes her husband would join her in Bible study and prayer, she has learned to live with a less than ideal situation. They are happy together.

After all, perhaps the influence of Clara's religion and life is beginning to make a difference. Recently Noelene and I dined with Ken and Clara and a few other friends. We ordered from the menu. It so happened that Ken was the only one to choose a salad, which was served before the other food. He sat with the food uneaten before him. We urged him to go ahead. We wondered why he, never a bashful man, seemed reluctant to eat. Then he spoke up: "I can't start until we have a blessing on the food!" Turning to me, he asked, "Would you say a grace for all of us?" Clearly Clara's Christian example is softening and changing Ken.

How Ken and Clara worked through their differences points to important principles if your spouse doesn't choose Adventism:

● **Preserve your marriage**

Two institutions set up by the Lord have come down to us from the Garden of Eden—the Sabbath and marriage. We make a promise to Jesus when we accept Him as Saviour and Lord, and that's the most serious and most important commitment we can ever make. But it doesn't cancel the promises we made at the wedding altar. If anything, choosing Adventism should make those promises more precious and binding.

When many of the early Christians accepted Jesus, their spouses remained in paganism. The apostle Paul addresses such people at length in 1 Corinthians 7.

These Christians apparently wondered whether their marriage still had validity. They were joined to Jesus Christ, but their spouses were not. How could the holy be linked with the unholy?

Paul assures the spouses of religiously divided households that their marriage is holy. Even though your partner is not a believer, he tells them, the union is made holy because of your commitment to the Lord. "For the unbelieving husband has been sanctified through his wife, and the unbelieving wife has been sanctified through her believing husband. Otherwise your children would be unclean, but as it is, they are holy" (1 Corinthians 7:14, NIV).

Being an Adventist should make us a better husband or wife. Because Jesus has forgiven us the enormous debt of our sins, we can be forgiving of others. Because He has shown us mercy and understanding, we can be merciful and understanding to our spouses. Because He suffers long with us, we can be more patient. Because we realize how far short we fall of His beauty and perfection of character, we can be more tolerant of our wife's or husband's faults.

● **Mutual respect**

To the sincere Adventist, our religious faith is the greatest thing in the world. It brings peace, contentment, fulfillment, and better health. It holds out the hope of endless life in the presence of our Saviour. Surely a person is unwise, even foolish, not to choose it!

But God gives to each of us freedom to choose. God respects that freedom—He doesn't compel us—and we must respect the individuality of our husband or wife who doesn't choose Adventism. We shouldn't look upon ourselves as better than they because they have not shared our choice.

● Working matters through

A good marriage needs open lines of communication. If a religious difference enters in, it's even more vital that you make a careful and earnest effort to understand each other.

If you have recently chosen Adventism, a new world is opening before you. Everything is changing—what you read, what you eat and drink, how you spend your time. You're even learning a new vocabulary. You begin to talk about the "message," the "truth," and "Sister White"!

As you are growing, you may grow away from your spouse unless you make a strong effort to help him or her understand what is happening. The problem is, he or she may not *want* to talk about your religion. Your marriage partner may still be smarting under your choice and may feel that any conversation about Adventism is simply a veiled means of converting him. Because of arguments and tensions that may have accompanied your decision to choose Adventism, you may find it easier quietly to avoid any attempt to explain what is happening.

But your marriage can come to grief unless you insist on reaching a basic understanding with each other. Make it clear to your spouse that you are not going to get into doctrinal matters again, but that you simply have to try to understand each other in areas like the handling of money, food, and entertainment.

I can't give you a formula for reaching such understandings. Certainly there is no need to try to resolve every issue at one sitting. Address the situations as they arise. As far as possible, try to anticipate problem areas and meet them ahead of time. Carefully and prayerfully seek for the most effective time and way to work matters through. And when you do, be quiet and patient and give more time to listening than to talking.

● **Retaining your individuality**

Respect is a two-way street. You should respect your spouse's right not to choose Adventism. Be flexible. Go the second mile to accommodate his or her wishes. But the Lord doesn't want you to lose your own individuality as you seek to please your mate.

Paul talked about this to those early Christians who were married to pagan spouses. He says that although your unbelieving partner is sanctified by your commitment to the Lord, He doesn't expect you to remain in the relationship if the situation becomes intolerable (see 1 Corinthians 7:12-16).

Your non-Adventist partner cannot forbid you to attend church, for instance. It isn't fair to demand that. Neither is it fair for him to insist that if you love him you will engage in sexual activities that violate your conscience.

God has made you both individuals. Marriage brings privileges and responsibilities—it's a joining of two bodies and minds in the closest relationship that life affords. It also means a giving up. If a marriage is to be successful, *both* partners must give in to the other, must yield to some degree. Yet at the same time both have to remain themselves, maintain discrete personalities, and retain their God-given individuality.

Working out a marriage relationship when your spouse has not chosen Adventism is simply an extension of this principle.

● **Have fun together**

Pastor Hyveth Williams, who conducts the Lonely Believer seminar, surveyed Adventists in and around Baltimore, Maryland, whose spouses aren't church members. She found that many of these lonely believers felt guilty about having a good time with their spouses. Any fun was suspect—even if they saw longtime Adventists indulging in it!

Carol and Jack had good times together. Wednesday nights they played cards with friends, weekends they'd watch a movie, and often they spent Saturday afternoons walking around a shopping mall.

But after five years of marriage Carol chose Adventism. And the fun stopped.

Jack wondered what had happened to the woman he loved. She no longer dressed attractively. She seemed to think it was a sin to laugh. She didn't want to have a good time anymore. She banned making love on Friday nights. The only thing she wanted to do was go to religious meetings.

Jack became very angry—with her, her church, and God. In fact, he hated God.

And Carol also felt unhappy. She knew Jack was angry, but her conscience wouldn't permit her to have fun with him.

Jack moved out—just across the street, but in with another woman!

Hurt and angry, Carol grew even more judgmental of Jack.

Then Carol showed up at the Lonely Believer seminar. What she learned opened her eyes. She began to realize that the breakup in the marriage wasn't, as she'd previously thought, all Jack's fault. She determined to try to win back his affection.

That would be difficult, she knew. Jack was so angry that he wouldn't even speak to her.

Carol began taking more pride in her appearance. She would dress modestly but nicely. She realized it wasn't a sin to buy perfume or to use makeup discreetly.

And she went out of her way to be nice to Jack. She knew what he liked and tried to please him. She found nonchurch activities that they could do together. She learned to have fun with him again.

Jack moved back. In fact, he moved so far that at the time of writing this book he's attending church with Carol.

What are some of the fun things that you can do with your non-SDA spouse? Here's a short list to give you a start. Then you can make your own.

Go camping, hiking, and mountain climbing together.
Listen to music together.
Go to symphonic or other musical concerts.
Eat out.
Enjoy parlor games.
Watch TV, rent a video (agree on parameters beforehand).
Take up sports—playing or watching.
Cook a meal together and invite friends over.

Let's look at some other areas you'll need to work through with your non-Adventist spouse.

Money

When we become Adventists, we see all that we are and have in a new light. We realize that we are stewards of all our time, influence, health, and possessions. Money in particular presents a problem to the non-Adventist spouse.

People who aren't Adventists, though members of other churches, simply don't understand how Adventists can return the tithe—the tenth of their increase—as well as give freewill offerings. They find this an enormous sum to give on a regular basis.

Of course, Christians who tithe regularly see it differently. To us tithing isn't an obligation, a demand of the church; rather, it's a grateful expression of our love for the Lord. And we find that the Lord, in ways that often seem miraculous, more than makes up the difference.

Your non-Adventist spouse likely will not see tithing as you do. You can explain tactfully and gently why the church recommends tithing, but you cannot insist that he or she tithes. You can encourage your marriage partner to pay a tithe, but don't get upset if he or she doesn't see the light.

Matters are simpler where each partner has a separate income. Your spouse may not choose to tithe, but he or she should not attempt to prevent you from doing so. Likewise, if you do not work, he or she should not attempt to prevent you from tithing the allowance that comes to you personally.

Even where both partners in a marriage share the same faith, matters of money often cause friction. In fact, marriage counselors cite disputes and misunderstandings over the use of money as one of the three chief factors leading to the breakup of American marriages. It's vital, therefore, that you and your spouse have a clear understanding about the way in which you both relate to the financial resources of the household.

Tithing led to friction in the home where I grew up. I was born during the depths of the Depression, the youngest of nine children. Good Anglican though she was, Mother couldn't see how Dad could take a tenth of his income and give it to the church when the children needed shoes and other items of clothing.

Though times are infinitely better today, tithing is still likely to trigger misunderstandings with your non-Adventist spouse.

Eating and Drinking

Adventists, seeking to glorify God in all that they do, for more than a century have recommended a simple lifestyle that includes abstinence from harmful products. Adventists don't drink or smoke, and they recommend a vegetarian diet as the most healthful.

For many years Adventists were a voice crying in the wilderness in matters of health. With dramatic suddenness, however, the scene has changed. Especially in North America, men and women by the millions have abandoned smoking. Today many people besides Adventists look upon tobacco as a drug, its use as a sign of weakness. More and more are turning away from alcohol also, although so far the numbers are far fewer than with tobacco.

And most people no longer consider vegetarianism odd. The United States surgeon general, concerned over the high incidence of heart disease, has recommended that Americans eat more fruit and vegetables, limit their intake of red meat, sugar, and salt. Millions of Americans have become vegetarians.

You may be one of the lucky ones whose spouse, although not an Adventist, has adopted a vegetarian diet. However, chances are that he or she hasn't. You have some tricky negotiating to do together.

Eating and drinking are highly personal. Mealtimes are social occasions, one of the hallmarks of civilized peoples. For many people, to suggest changes in these areas is like laying a hand on their persons.

Here is our suggestion: be firm in essentials but be flexible in nonessentials.

For example, many items of diet, although not recommended in the Adventist lifestyle, need not offend conscience. Acquaint your spouse with the benefits of vegetarianism and learn how to prepare tasteful nonmeat dishes—they require skill. But don't require that he give up meat altogether. You needn't feel obligated to eat meat dishes placed on the table, but inasmuch as meat is not specifically forbidden in the Scriptures, you should respect his dietary preferences.

Likewise with tea and coffee. The Seventh-day Adventist Church recommends that members abstain from them because of their caffeine content. You should; but you shouldn't withhold them from your spouse if he or she wants to have them.

Can two people with radically different dietary preferences enjoy each other's company? Yes, indeed. As I travel among people who aren't Christians, I find quite a few who are vegetarians. They get along fine with others. And given love, mutual respect, and good humor, an Adventist and a non-Adventist spouse can learn to make mealtimes fun.

What if your spouse smokes and/or drinks? As distasteful as the practice may be to you, you must respect your mate's freedom of choice. Put the thought out of your mind that you will not love or respect him or her unless the habit is discontinued. Accept your marriage partner as he or she is. Keep love blossoming.

Worship

You love Sabbath school and church, camp meetings—any Adventist gathering. On these occasions, which increasingly become the most precious moments in your life, you desire above all else that your spouse might be with you.

Invite him or her to join you, and keep on inviting even though you get a negative answer. The day may come when your spouse will decide to come out to a particular function—to a concert, to hear a special speaker, to a General Conference session.

If your mate belongs to another denomination and attends church on a regular basis, the situation is easier. Try to work out an arrangement whereby, respecting each other's beliefs, you go to church together—on both Sabbaths and Sundays.

Winning Your Spouse

The apostle Peter gives wives of nonbelieving partners some good advice: "Wives, in the same way be submissive to your husbands so that, if any of them do not believe the word, they may be won over without talk by the behavior of their wives, when they see the purity and reverence of your lives" (1 Peter 3:1, 2, NIV).

What if your spouse knows what you believe and why but still has not decided for Adventism? Badgering is of no use. Let your life of loving, gentle behavior be your means of witness.

Never give up living that life. Never give up praying for him or her. Never give up hoping.

And over the years a spouse may change in subtle ways that you do not discern. He or she may, as a result of your influence, come to consider himself or herself an Adventist.

Some years ago Noelene and I went out one Sunday to a

U-pick orchard. When the man in charge greeted us, he asked if we were Adventists. We told him that we were, and he replied, "We're also Adventists."

After we had picked our fruit, weighed it, paid for it, and were about to leave, we met his wife. "I'm an Adventist, but my husband isn't," she confided. In fact, she seemed to want us to understand very clearly that he wasn't an Adventist!

Noelene and I have often wondered whether that woman had failed to notice where her husband found his identity, or whether her understanding of Adventism had led her to believe that she must drive a wedge between them. Whatever the reason, we went away surprised—and more than a little disappointed.

In this chapter we have tried to look at the main areas that can cause conflict between the person who has chosen Adventism and that person's non-Adventist spouse. So far we have not talked about the children—when they don't choose Adventism or when they alone of the family do. That topic deserves its own treatment in a separate chapter.

3

Your Children

Like changing the rules in the middle of a game, the conversion of parents to Adventism could seem unfair and uncalled-for to children. How well the children accept the changes depends upon the parents, the children, and the relationship existing between them.

Lynn Bratcher works with Noelene at the General Conference headquarters. Lynn describes her former way of life as that of a "swinging single." Dissatisfied with the direction of her life, she turned to the Bible and discovered the Seventh-day Adventist Church. How did 23-year-old Greg and 14-year-old Linda react to their mother's change of lifestyle?

"They didn't mind what I did," Lynn explains. "They just didn't plan to change their own lives." And Lynn didn't try to change them. She respected their right to choose for themselves.

Had Lynn's children been younger, still in their formative years when they accepted her as the all-knowing authority figure in their lives, she could more easily have turned their footsteps in a new direction. A child's age influences the approach a parent will use in helping the child to choose Adventism.

Switching to an Adventist lifestyle is likely to uncover a host of sticky situations for a child. Sitting still in church, for instance, seems like a stupendous undertaking to a wriggly

4-year-old who has never been required to sit and listen before. Leaving the television off on Sabbath could be just as difficult at any age. A 7-year-old fussy eater facing a whole new diet, a prissy 9-year-old forgoing pierced ears, an aspiring Little Leaguer facing the prospect of summer without Friday night and Sabbath baseball—the list of possible catastrophes is endless.

How did they do it—those parents who joined the church with their families intact? Whatever the particular circumstances of a family, one fact emerges: children ultimately join Adventism the way adults do—because they choose it.

How to Influence the Choice

Parents may do much to encourage a positive choice, especially if they begin early. The sooner children experience the sweet influence of Christ's love, the easier the task of helping them choose Jesus. Why? Because the younger the child, and the less firmly cemented the habits, the easier the change.

Whatever the age of a child, remember that love is the best motivator of change. Very young children don't fully understand who God is; they equate parental love with God's love. And because their parents love God and want to please Him, little children will try to obey Him too.

But it's still difficult to always "be good" when you are 7 years old—it's hard enough when you're 37! But although we can't remake ourselves, Jesus can transform us. And what's more, He wants to make us "good." When we turn things over to Him and spend time reading the Bible and talking to Him, good things begin to happen. Personal prayer and Bible study allow God time to work on our hearts and to change our lives.

Prayer and Bible study helped our children, also. All the hours that we spent reading *The Bible Story* books to Terry and Julie weren't just keeping them out of mischief. We were giving the Lord an opportunity to forge bonds of love that will last a lifetime.

One evening Noelene detected a note of special love and concern in Terry's prayers. Next day she noticed the extra effort he put forth to be kind and good. It kept up for five days. At the weekend she discovered that George Maywald, a dear family friend and minister of the gospel, had been partly responsible for the change. He had taken time out of his busy schedule to conduct special Week of Prayer worships at the church school. The Lord never wastes the extra time we devote to Him. We know; we saw the life of a second-grader change in one week.

Of course, the change in its full intensity didn't last all that long. It never does. But that doesn't mean that a person is bad or that he or she has not chosen to follow the Lord. It merely points up the frailty of human nature. As a person continues in the Christian way—practicing daily prayer and Bible study—patterns of behavior change and the change becomes permanent.

"Bible reading and prayer are the keys with teens, too," Lynn says. Nobody can chart a course for others to follow that will guarantee the salvation of their children. After all, children also have a choice in the matter. But whether your child is a committed Christian or not, "constant kneeling" is the best means of influencing that choice. Lynn recommends the book *The Kneeling Christian,* available at Christian bookstores.

Bobby was a member of Lynn's youth Sabbath school group. He had grown up Adventist but had fallen in with a bad crowd. He confessed to Lynn that he couldn't shake his teenage drinking habit.

"I remembered how I used to love partying," Lynn recalls. "I hadn't done anything in particular to break the partying habit. But the Bible had become so relevant to me that I wanted to study it every spare moment."

One day a friend asked Lynn, "When did you give up

partying and dancing?" Lynn couldn't remember. She had been too busy with her new Friend and her new faith. This gave Lynn an idea to try on Bobby.

"Don't worry about the drinking problem for now," she advised. "Just promise me that you will take time every morning and night to read the Bible and pray. Concentrate on getting to know Jesus as your friend." Bobby followed Lynn's advice and gradually his drinking problem disappeared.

Teenagers may be influenced to choose Adventism by an adult friend or counselor like Lynn or by their parents. But there's a mysterious fact about Christianity—you must accept it wholeheartedly, unreservedly, before you can lead others to choose it. So before talking to teenagers about their need for Jesus, be sure to practice constant prayer yourself. If you have that vital connection with the Lord, He will infuse your witness with power—drawing power.

And remember, the Lord needs your help in answering your prayers for your children. Working together, parents and God make a formidable team!

After the Choice, Sainthood?

Joining the Seventh-day Adventist Church should not mean that children suddenly have a discouragingly high standard of behavior to attain. Rather, it means that they have a better reason for wanting to set their goals high and a better means of achieving them.

"Parents must never discourage or shame children," Lynn Bratcher urges. Harsh words are like icy April winds that brown the petals of the tulip tree. Effective Christian parenting begins and ends with unconditional love, the mild breeze that coaxes spirituality into bloom.

Lynn's son, Greg, was 23 when he accepted Adventism. He had begun attending a Sundaykeeping church. But he had many bad habits that worried her. "I had no right to force my new values on him," Lynn explains. "But he was worrying me. I badly wanted him to choose a drug-free life with Jesus."

Lynn tried cajoling and lecturing, but it was spoiling the relationship between them. One day after turning Greg over to the Lord, she faced Greg with the problem. She explained once more the damage that drugs were doing to his body.

"This is your choice," she said. "It's OK with me. But I don't want you out with criminals. If you have to do it, do it at home, here in your room. It's your body, and you have many years to put up with it. I can't stop you."

"While it was my mother's problem, I didn't think much about what I was doing," Greg says. "But when she put it on my shoulders, I had to take another look and see if this was really what I wanted."

Greg began taking an interest in his mother's new ideas. Soon he too chose Adventism. Other parents may not choose to do exactly as Lynn did, especially if they have younger children at home. But God promises to help you handle the problem wisely.

Linda was slower to make her decision. She had always been easily influenced by good, but choosing a church that put her at odds with her friends and community was a difficult step for a 14-year-old. Lynn tried not to force her decision on Linda, either, and soon her daughter began studying Adventism with her mother.

Sometimes we church members are too impatient to see new believers look and act like us. The members of Lynn's church were no exception.

"One day a group of Adventist women were meeting at my house," Lynn remembers. "Linda asked me to drive her and a friend to a movie."

Lynn wondered what to do. She couldn't give up her responsibilities as a parent. Linda had not yet accepted Adventism fully, and saw nothing wrong with watching a good movie. Not wanting to force Adventist values on her daughter, Lynn quietly explained where she was going, and excused herself from the women's group. One of the Adventists clearly showed her disapproval. But Lynn refused to feel guilty because of her daughter's choice. A few months later Linda gave up worldly dress and amusements and asked to be baptized.

So now that the key choice had been made, Lynn's problems with Linda were over, right? Wrong. "I then had to face all the normal problems that Adventist parents face," she told me recently. Dating, dress, and curfew were but some of the areas in which decisions were constantly made and standards tested.

"We must remember that teens, even if they have been brought up in the church, are still baby Christians," Lynn advises. Just as a good parent anticipates the needs of a baby, so parents and leaders should think and plan for youthful Christians.

Lynn volunteered to help her church's youth group. Sharon Presgrove, the thirtyish youth leader, owned a van. "We bundled those dozen kids into that van and trundled them all over the state of Oklahoma," Lynn chuckles. "Sharon was terrific. She was determined that the kids would feel positive about being Adventist. We didn't miss an event that a Christian could enjoy."

The peer group in that predominantly Baptist town enjoyed dancing and drinking. "The Baptist church also fought the drinking," Lynn says. To replace the dancing, Sharon substituted cookouts at the lake, well-chaperoned sleepouts, campouts, and games in the evenings. Lynn served nonalcoholic sparkling grape juice in place of the booze.

Sharon encouraged four kids who had never sung before to practice as a quartet. They provided special music and gave their testimonies when the group visited other Adventist churches. The kids were growing in the Christian way and having fun, too.

Standards for Teens

Teens are still learning about Adventist standards. So when trying to uphold standards, we should follow a course similar to one we might advocate for brand-new Adventists. Here are some steps to remember:

● **Emphasize Bible study and prayer as a means for establishing a right relationship with God.**

This relationship is more important than learning about the fine points of doctrine. Ellen White should be introduced as an author whose books help one to grow in one's relationship with Jesus. *Steps to Christ* is a good book to read first.

● **Explain the principles from which Adventist standards spring.**

Never say "You should do it this way because the church [or the *Church Manual*] says so." Give *your* reason for accepting the standard.

● **Having explained the principle, allow teens time and space to make their choice.**

Don't keep pressuring them with your point of view. And prepare to accept your teen's choice—whatever it is.

● **Resort to prayer.**

Of course, you have been praying all along. But you need prayer more than ever now. It's hard to let go and allow a responsible teen to make an independent decision. Be sure to pray, not that your teen will accept *your* choice, but that he or she will hold fast to the relationship with Jesus. And pray twice as often for the softening influence of complete surrender in your own life. Believe me, this works. It helped Noelene and me guide two young Christians into their early twenties.

● **Don't accept guilt for the choices made by your growing Christians.**

And don't apologize for them to other church members. When a church member doesn't approve of your child or understand something a teen has done, the problem is not yours but that member's. (Pray that God will never let you forget what it's like to bring up young Christians!)

● **Teach teens that they are accountable to God for their behavior—not to parents or other church members.**

If they feel accountable to you, they can mask their outward behavior to fool you, but they can't fool God.

● **Rather than outlawing unacceptable pleasures, replace them.**

And if possible, anticipate problems before they arise. Keep kids busy having good, clean, constructive fun.

● **Don't forbid teens to make friends with non-Adventists.**

Draw the non-Adventists into the fellowship of your youth group, as long as they don't cause a split in the group or openly challenge your authority. Be cautious about turning anyone away from your group.

● **Try not to throw up imaginary barriers between youth and other people.**

Jesus came to show us how to live in the world. The Pharisees came up with the idea of drawing one's garments close and keeping the world at bay. Jesus drew all people to Him; so should we.

Nobody can tell you how to handle each situation that arises. The above principles are a good guide, but they leave much up to your judgment.

For instance, little children follow simple do's and don'ts without question. They aren't particularly interested in reasons. Teens demand a good reason and the right to choose. So how do you know when to switch from telling to advising?

Offer good reasons from the earliest years whether children seem interested or not. Knowing that your child could demand the right to make most decisions by age 15, provide early opportunities for decision-making under your guidance. Gradually change your approach as your child grows up.

In our enthusiasm to help others accept our lifestyle, we must remember that people, like sheep, cannot be commanded in the way they should go. They must be led. Leading children means encouraging them to do what must be done rather than ordering them to do it.

But what do we do with the children who don't respond to our efforts, who don't fit the mold?

Jimmy had not often been restrained as a little boy. When my Auntie Madge and 5-year-old Jimmy began attending church, he mortified her. He was active and funny, but awfully disruptive. The church members treated Jimmy as if he were bad, and eventually Auntie Madge stopped bringing him to church. What might have been done to keep Jimmy in church and help him change?

First, we must reassure both Jimmy and Auntie Madge that there is no bad child. There's really no good child, either. All children are a mixture of both. Child training is a name for the task of bringing out the good in children and making rightdoing pleasant, rewarding, and habitual.

Keeping this in mind, the pastor might have had a quiet talk with Jimmy and offered him a simple, concrete reward for sitting still in church. He might also have remembered Jimmy's needs and provided more opportunity for children to move around—like inviting them to sit up front for a story prior to the sermon. A word of encouragement after church each Sabbath might have helped. Any friendly member could say, "It's hard sitting through church, but you're growing up fast. Next week if you feel like you can't sit still, you may come and sit by me."

Praising and encouraging grown-up behavior work wonders. Besides, children respond to the friendly notice of adults. As a resentful eighth grader, Noelene responded to Mrs. Dempsey's encouragement. She always greeted her and often found ways that Noelene could help with the church music. Noelene would have done anything for Mrs. Dempsey.

When our children reached the age when they looked for adult attention, Noelene despaired of any "Mrs. Dempsey" discovering them. How we wished that adults today would interact with the children and teenagers as Mrs. Dempsey did. We couldn't create a Mrs. Dempsey for our children, neither can you. But we can be a Mrs. Dempsey and fill a real need for other children and teens.

If love and encouragement don't work and behavior is truly worrisome, parents may need to resort to punishment. But try to fit punishments to the misdeeds and keep spankings as a last resort. Try constantly to avoid trouble rather than to be always mopping up afterward.

How to Face Opposition

Often new believers face opposition to their new way of life from family and friends. While opposition is never pleasant, it helps Christians strengthen their resolve. But this offers little comfort to children. Here are some suggestions to help children weather adverse reactions:

● **Recognize the problem.**

Don't say, "Oh, it can't be that bad" or "Try to ignore it" when a child complains about opposition. Instead, face the problem with your child. Ask him or her to tell you what happened. Admit that the incident must have been disagreeable.

● **Try to understand how the child feels.**

Suppose that a teacher belittles Tom because he cannot attend the Friday evening dance. After Tom describes what happened, say, "You must have felt terrible. Didn't you feel angry? You must have wished you could punch somebody."

● **Offer encouragement.**

Praise Tom for enduring the embarrassment. If he did not, in fact, react well, sympathize with his embarrassment at having let God down. Reassure him that God will help him do better next time. Plan something significant that the family can do with Tom that will help make up for what he will miss.

Living With a No Vote

Suppose that you have tried everything to influence your teenager to choose Adventism and adjust to the new lifestyle, but he or she resolutely turns it all down. What can you do then?

You have three basic choices: (1) force him to conform while he lives under your roof; (2) turn him out of the house; or (3) come to an understanding, a compromise, that will allow the family to maintain its loving, accepting atmosphere.

The first two options seem uncharacteristic of Christianity. The kingdom of heaven, after all, is based on freedom to choose. Nowhere in the Bible does God force Himself on people. Whatever our reaction to Him, He goes on loving us. And nowhere does the Bible admonish Christian parents to turn their home into a battlefield in their crusade for the cause. Jesus offers peace. Homes are to be a little bit of heaven—a safe harbor from strife.

Because children under 10 tend to follow their parents' example and conform to their wishes, the problem of how to handle the child who rejects Adventism is a problem involving older children. Exactly how to work out the details depends on the age of the children and whether both parents are Adventist.

In working out a compromise in lifestyle so that the whole family can live harmoniously, include the following:

- **Respect your teenager's right not to choose Adventism.**
- **Encourage your teenager to be the best of whatever he or she chooses to be.**
- **Encourage your teenager to choose and follow a high moral code of conduct and to accept responsibility for his or her actions.**
- **Expect children to obey rules that any decent family might set.**

But do not try to legislate an Adventist lifestyle. Any family has a right to outlaw acid rock in their home, for instance. But allowing only classical music would be going too far.

Provided teens conform to school rules and what is generally considered decent by society, a parent really has no right to force teens against their will to dress in any particular fashion.

● **Stand together on family rules.**

Parents should discuss any rule they disagree on until they find a compromise. Suppose you wish to ban movie attendance for your non-Adventist child, but your spouse objects. You may compromise with a family rule that states: no movie attendance without at least one parent's approval of the movie.

● **Don't give up on a nonbelieving child.**

Though you may wish that he or she had chosen differently in regard to religion or any other aspect of his life, assure your child of your approval of him as a person. Nothing discourages a person or saps ambition like the nagging reminder that he or she does not measure up to parental expectations. Go on loving and accepting regardless of the child's choice, just as Jesus does.

● **Emphasize what you and the nonbelieving child have in common; minimize differences.**

Although Murray has been brought up in an Adventist home, he has never chosen to join the church through baptism. His parents could nag him on this point by reminding him that officially he is not a member of the church. But if they notice all that Murray does to help people in need, they will rejoice that he is so close to the ideal.

● **Accept your teenager's choice.**

Stop trying to change his mind. Turn him over to God and try to enjoy what is left to you.

● **Don't carry a load of guilt for your unbelieving children.**

He or she is responsible to God, not you. Don't worry about what might have been. Heredity and environment, while greatly influencing one's choices, do not make the final decision.

Remember, there's no limit to the fragrance and influence of a godly life. So go on living in the joy of the Lord. Trust Him to work out a satisfactory conclusion in His time, His way.

4

Relating to Family Members

We'll really miss you and Lisa in the choir next Sabbath," Noelene told Carla after Wednesday's choir practice at Greater Nashville Junior Academy. "But I'm glad you have chosen to be baptized."

The school's Christmas baptism was celebrated in a special way by all the students, especially those in fourth through eighth grades. Choir specials, an eighth-grade girls' trio, and the fourth-grade flute ensemble had been polished with anticipation. But nobody looked forward to the baptism with more joy than Carla and Lisa.

Their dad had turned away from Adventism in his teens as a protest against the exacting requirements of religion that he had experienced. He had married out of the church but had brought up his two girls well. In this, their first year in an Adventist school, they were sincere and wide-eyed in their acceptance of the truths presented in Bible class. More than anything else, they longed to seal their commitment to Adventism by being baptized. So it was with some shock that Noelene heard Carla say, "But we *will* be singing in the choir next Sabbath. We're not going to be baptized. We're going to wait for our daddy and be baptized as a family."

Afraid that they may have been stalled as a way of changing their commitment, Noelene could only murmur, "I hope you are doing the right thing." But she need not have worried. Someone far wiser than she was guiding the girls.

Within a few months their father recommitted his life to the Lord, and the whole family was baptized together.

For those who make a serious commitment to Adventism, as Carla and Lisa did, their Lord comes first. And then they instinctively reach out to those they love, longing for them to enjoy the freedom and exhilaration that complete surrender brings.

But unfortunately families do not always respond as Carla's did. How do we cope with the day-to-day realities of living in a family that neither welcomes nor understands Adventism? How do we help loved ones appreciate the changes in our outlook and lifestyle? How do we keep family ties close while at the same time keeping our spiritual life strong?

For here is the sad fact: *most families survive a member's becoming a Christian, but many break up if one becomes an Adventist.* Genuine Adventism calls for a drastic change of lifestyle. Unless relationships are handled carefully and positively, the gospel of Jesus—which He intended to bring reconciliation—can divide a family.

Carla's family teaches us two lessons.

First, it's worth it to patiently work for whole families, delaying one's baptism if necessary to show one's concern for parental authority or to accompany another family member in the path to full commitment to Jesus. Even more important, Carla's dad taught me to respect the spiritual journey of others.

Our two families had accompanied the Pathfinders of Nashville's First church on a camping weekend at Indian Creek. After a busy Sunday morning we joined the girls' parents in a quiet paddle around the lake. In the course of our conversation, we mentioned how we feared for some of our family and friends who had not committed themselves to the Lord or the church.

"I never worry about that," James said. "I have learned to leave those worries with the Lord. He alone knows where we each stand in relation to Him. He alone can save. So I just commit my friends to God and ask Him to care for them. And I trust them to serve Him in their own way."

If you have chosen Adventism for the first time or have recommitted your life to Jesus in a new, deeper way and yearn for your family or close friends to find the Lord as you have, what can you do for them? Here are a few suggestions:

● **Respect their views and their concept of God.**

You show respect by listening to the other person's opinions and by trying to find common beliefs. You can always find something to agree on.

When my brother Gordon talks of his belief that one's moral values should be based on Christian principles, I agree with him. I don't point out that I believe Christian principles should be based on the commandments—all *ten* of them! If Gordon wants to discuss the Sabbath, he'll bring it up. And until he does, we'll stick to common ground.

People tend to avoid those who get preachy in their conversation. On the other hand, everyone enjoys the reassurance that comes with a nod and a sincere "I think so too."

And here's a *don't.* Don't hold your family hostage to your emotions. Without saying it, you can convey the impression: "I won't love you as much if you don't keep Sabbath with me" or "I won't value you as before if you keep on smoking."

● **Be a good advertisement for your beliefs.**

Have you noticed how advertising agencies make products inviting? They select youthful, healthful, beautiful models who radiate happiness and confidence. And one of Adventism's wisest authors wrote: "Christians should be the most cheerful and happy people that live" *(Messages to Young People,* p. 363).

When invited to eat, drink, or do something that you cannot share with a clear conscience, instead of shyly refusing on the grounds that you are a new Adventist, say, "How sweet of you to offer. I used to enjoy [whatever], but I've chosen a whole new lifestyle. I feel so much better not indulging in [whatever]. But you go ahead. I'll [name something you'll enjoy doing or eating]." Or suggest something that you can both enjoy together.

Resist the urge to launch into a defense of your reasoning—unless the other person invites you to. In that case, if you can't remember the Bible texts that impressed you to change your habits (such as 1 Corinthians 6:19, 20—your body is God's temple; 1 Corinthians 10:31—do all to God's glory; or Philippians 4:8—do whatever is true, noble, right, pure, lovely, and admirable), offer to provide them at a later time. Be sure to link your reasoning to your intense love for the Saviour. Unless motivated by love, your actions will seem purely legalistic to an observer.

And remember, what you *are* is far more important than what you say. Your sensitivity to the love that motivates the invitations and offers that you must turn down is more important than the yes or no response. Only a close relationship with God can help you glide over these hurdles. Renew your commitment to God every morning, and pray to be molded into a positive, living advertisement for truth.

● **The Christian lifestyle speaks for itself.**

By consistently and faithfully living a balanced Christian life, you allow the Lord to demonstrate His power through you. Noelene's eyes were opened to this when she was searching for professional photographs to use in the central exhibit that surrounded the lighted globe at the General Conference session in New Orleans.

Her committee easily located pictures to illustrate a young, caring family that could pass as Adventists. The problem was to find a picture of a retired couple. Picture after picture from the stock files posed no problems in style of dress or lack of adornment, but the committee rejected them because of the skin condition of the face.

"Surely this one is right," my wife suggested, thinking she had solved the problem. But the professional designer rejected it. "Look at the skin around the eyes," he said. "She looks like a reformed alcoholic!" It's true. Longtime Seventh-day Adventists have better skin, more youthful faces.

Unfortunately, Adventists can sometimes also look more stern. How we live and think affects how we look and feel. The more healthfully we eat and exercise, the better we will look and feel—provided we enjoy life and are motivated by a deep and continuing love for God. After all, He makes the changes in us.

Many of us find it hard to decide for a healthful diet when the foods we must give up taste so good. But most people want to look good and enjoy themselves. If people see that our lifestyle makes us happier and more attractive, they may want to find out what makes the difference and try it too.

● **Keep family ties strong.**

Having someone in a family who believes and acts differently from the rest is like having a burr in your sock, a stone in your shoe, or grit in your cornflakes. The first reaction is to get rid of it. Parents may interpret the burr as a threat to their authority and try to compensate for it by being more strict. Brothers and sisters may think that they can talk the offender out of his crazy ideas. You can expect unpleasant arguments.

When these efforts don't help, family unity becomes severely strained. The family begins to question the new Adventist's love and loyalty.

Ruthie minimized such misunderstandings by going out of her way to obey and love her parents. She worked extra-hard around the house so that her parents wouldn't be inconvenienced by her absence from home on Saturday mornings. At every opportunity she verbalized her love for them. When she couldn't comply with their wishes, she expressed her sorrow and reaffirmed her respect for them. Eventually they had to admit that Ruthie was a better daughter. Her mother decided to discover what had made the difference.

● **Communicate that it's OK if your relatives don't choose Adventism.**

Having chosen Adventism, we know we've found pure gold. We so much want our loved ones to find it too. We also sense that church members are hoping to see us win the family for Christ and the church.

But we can't decide for them—and they may choose otherwise. Then it's easy for us to become embarrassed over them when we are around other Adventists.

How will we feel if our friends from church see us walking down the street with someone who is smoking? Or if they meet us in a restaurant, dining with someone who has ordered wine with his meal?

The easy response is to have less to do with our relatives who don't measure up to Adventist standards. We want to avoid introducing them to our "clean" Adventist friends.

That's the easy way—but it's wrong. By such actions we indicate that we do not value our loved ones as we once did. The subtle or not-so-subtle message is "You aren't good enough to be in the company of my friends."

Janice lived in London with her mother and sister. All three were Christians, all churchgoers.

Then Janice chose Adventism. She was excited about what she'd found. She knew Adventism should make a difference to a person—inside and outside. She went home and, she says, "literally forced my family to cook, to dress, and to talk as I did."

They resented it. If this was Adventism, they wanted none of it.

Janice meant well and was disappointed. But slowly she came to see that whether or not her mother and sister accepted her faith, they were special, important in their own right. She would pray for them and work for them, but it was OK if they didn't join her. She would accept them as she did before.

After some time Janice moved to the United States and

settled in Michigan. When her mother came to visit her, Janice introduced her to the conference president and other leaders of the church. She loves her mom and is proud of her. She states, "I'd show her off even if she had 10 heads."

Janice's mother was surprised. She'd expected her daughter to be embarrassed to bring her out among the Adventists. On the first few occasions when introduced, she said, "I'm not an Adventist; I'm a Baptist." She needed to say it to maintain her sense of identity. Janice didn't comment on it.

One day when they went to lunch, Janice introduced her by saying, "This is my mother. She's from London and she's a Baptist." Afterward she asked Janice, "Aren't you embarrassed to tell people I'm not an Adventist?"

"No, Mom, *you* are important to me. I don't care what you are."

"Well, why don't you show me why you believe worshiping on Saturday is the right thing?" the woman suggested.

That was the first time she had inquired about Janice's beliefs. It was, says Janice, "because I'd said, 'You are OK to me as you are.' "

Janice's mother joined the church after she returned to London.

● **Identify the major issues that you are willing to fight for.**

Glenda and Matt chose Adventism after marriage. They were almost overwhelmed with all the details of their new lifestyle that differed from the norm of their non-Seventh-day Adventist families. Not wishing to spoil the loving relationships of a lifetime, they decided to identify the most important principles of Christian living and fight for them. They would give in on minor points rather than turn family visits into battles.

Because vegetarianism posed a major problem when they visited their families, they explained their new diet but agreed to eat a little chicken or fish while at home. When Glenda's mother saw how hard the children tried to eat what was set before them, though they genuinely disliked it, she looked up a vegetarian cookbook and provided dishes that both sides of the family could enjoy. "But they would rather have not invited us to a meal than change their eating habits, until we showed that we were willing to adjust," Glenda says.

Dan and Roberta agonized over whether to attend a family reunion on Sabbath. To stay away would have given the signal that family ties no longer mattered. The family would then have concluded that the church had broken up a happy family.

"We prayed with the children and discussed the matter beforehand," Roberta says. "We went for the meal and managed to spend a few minutes with each relative, expressing our interest in them." When the party warmed up after dinner and the younger generation brought out their rock records, Dan and Roberta quietly took their family home.

Nobody can lay down a set of rules to help you negotiate the shoals of interpersonal relationships. We each have to think through the pros and cons of relating with non-Adventist families, confident that the One who has brought us thus far will guide us on to a happy conclusion.

5

Study, Work, Play

I studied for my doctoral degree at Vanderbilt University in Nashville, Tennessee. I was the first Seventh-day Adventist to be admitted into the New Testament program, and the professors knew from the beginning about my Adventist identity. To my good fortune, these men and women were practicing Christians who respected my beliefs and expected that I would contribute a unique perspective to the doctoral seminars and discussions.

Some of the students in the program were a different matter, however. Early on I had the impression that one or two looked askance at me, skeptical that a Seventh-day Adventist would be able to hold his own in the vigorous and at times brutal rough-and-tumble of doctoral studies.

That first semester I enrolled in a seminar dealing with law, grace, and freedom in the New Testament. Each week several students prepared short papers on assigned biblical passages. They distributed copies of these papers in advance of the seminar, and we were all expected to come to the seminar prepared to critique—which usually meant tearing apart—the papers and to discuss the passages.

The second or third week one of the papers dealt with Mark 2:23-28, the well-known passage that ends, "Therefore the Son of man is Lord also of the sabbath." As I read the student's paper prepared on this passage, I knew the forthcoming seminar would be a lively one. After making a brief exegesis of the passage, the student in his conclusions stated that it was certain that none of the early Christians kept the Sabbath!

After much prayer I came to the seminar, my mental guns loaded to discharge a salvo of New Testament passages that opposed the student's conclusion. But the discussion took a course I had not expected.

In harmony with the procedure for the seminar, the student first made a brief presentation. The professor followed with analysis and comments and then opened the paper to critique by class members. There was a pause. I drew a deep breath, about to challenge the concluding paragraphs of the paper.

But just before I opened my mouth, another student spoke up. "I have a problem with this paper," he said. "Its conclusions simply won't hold water."

The student presenter looked startled, a flush starting to spread over his face. His fellow student went on: "For instance, when he says that it's certain that none of the early Christian churches kept the Sabbath, he is ignoring important New Testament data. We know that the Christians whom Matthew addressed in his gospel kept the Sabbath. Matthew 24:20 makes that clear. Mr. P______ needs to revise his paper."

Other students joined the fray, supporting the student critic and challenging other aspects of the paper. I sat back. Without a word from me, my fellow students had vindicated the Sabbath from the New Testament!

After that seminar I noticed a change in the student who had been grilled that morning. He was less condescending in his attitude toward me, more respectful of my opinions and beliefs. His attitude softened still further at the end of the course, when to his amazement he learned that I was the only one to earn an A grade for the seminar. Over the next two years we became good friends.

My doctoral studies taught me that a Seventh-day Adventist who knows his Bible can hold his own in any company. From the outset of my time at Vanderbilt, I determined that I would be true to the Scriptures, allowing the text to confront me starkly and openly, letting the chips fall where they might. This, it seemed to me, was in keeping with the best traditions of Adventism. Our pioneers were men and women who took the Bible seriously, who were prepared to follow its teachings no matter how difficult they might prove to be.

And I quickly discovered that my Adventist background in the Scriptures was an advantage rather than a disadvantage. True, I was far less acquainted with the writings of Bultmann and other scholars than my fellow students; but to my surprise I found that some of them had an extremely poor knowledge of the Scriptures. When during close study of the Word I would point out allusions to other parts of the New Testament—to the obvious appreciation of the professors—some of my fellow doctoral candidates would look up perplexed, unable to follow the gist of the discussion.

The Lord was marvelously good to me in that program. He brought me through my doctoral degree much faster than any of those who were admitted with me.

Some of you who read this book may also find yourself in a non-Adventist study setting. I strongly support Seventh-day Adventist education at all levels, but for various reasons Adventists, whether newly converted to the faith or not, may find themselves studying in a non-Adventist school. I suggest this: be yourself. Stand tall in your individuality. Maintain your Adventist identity.

The Lord wants us to be pleasant, positive witnesses for Him. I think we serve Him best by simply being what we are. Confident, but not pushy. Sure of ourselves, but not preachy.

Some Adventists I know like to introduce themselves with "I'm proud to be a Seventh-day Adventist." That may be fine for them, and I don't want to discourage them from their own style of representing the Lord, but it wouldn't sound right from my lips.

Whatever sounds right to you, say it. Be yourself—a person consecrated to the Lord. Hold your head high as a Seventh-day Adventist. Our faith in all its aspects—teachings, mission, lifestyle—can stand the severest scrutiny.

My studies at Vanderbilt University convinced me of that. They demonstrated to me that Seventh-day Adventism is closer to early Christianity than is any other denomination.

At Work

Some people confuse the call to follow Jesus with the call to be a full-time church worker. They discover Adventism and in their enthusiasm feel ready to leave their work and take up studies for the ministry. After all, if Jesus is coming back soon, why fool around with secular employment? Didn't Saul of Tarsus do the same? When he met Jesus on the Damascus road and gave his heart to Him, didn't he leave his former work to take up preaching the gospel?

No, Saul—who became Paul—didn't do so immediately. He had much to learn and much to unlearn before the Lord could use him to be the founder of the Gentile mission. The Lord first sent Paul to Arabia, preparing him gradually for the tasks He had mapped out for him (see Galatians 1:17).

People newly converted to Adventism also need time to sort things out and be sure the Lord really is calling them into full-time service. Obviously, the great majority of Adventists cannot be employed by the church. They are to serve the Lord as faithful laymen and laywomen, sharing their faith in the workplace and in the marketplace.

The Lord Jesus employed a series of symbols to illustrate what He wants us to be in the world. You are to be salt, He said, giving a good taste to society. You are to be yeast, He said, working silently to leaven the whole lump of society. You are to be light, He said, rolling back the darkness in your neighborhood and in your workplace (Matthew 5:13-16; 13:33).

In many respects it's easier to work for the church. You don't have to rub shoulders with men and women who smoke, drink, and swear. You don't have to face questions about why you don't eat this or that, or why you don't do this or that. You can have times of worship together. You share a common mission and a common hope.

But the Lord calls us not to an easy life, but to follow *Him*. Following Jesus means that for most of us our work will be in the world. Jesus didn't shut Himself off from society. He didn't gather a band of people around Himself and go off into the sticks to form a commune where everybody would dress alike, eat alike, speak alike, and smell alike. No, Jesus went where the people were. Although from time to time He drew apart to pray—at times spending the whole night speaking to His Father—He spent most of His time out among the people. Wherever someone was hurting, wherever someone was sick, wherever someone was crying, that's where Jesus went.

And so must we.

When we understand our work aright, it is worship. For the Adventist, all that we do is to the glory of God. The lay members who work faithfully and well in their Adventist identity witness for the Lord just as surely as does the preacher who stands before thousands on Sabbath mornings. But lay people influence people who will never go to hear the preacher.

Several years ago the Catholic Church in France witnessed a remarkable development. Many priests laid aside their cassocks, left their churches, put on working clothes, and found their place among the workers of Paris. No, these priests hadn't renounced Catholicism; rather, tired of ministering in empty churches and concerned that the life of the church seemed ever more distant from the life of the workers, they decided to take their place in the factories of France.

They became known as the worker-priests. They would seek to minister to men and women by meeting them on the job.

Adventists contact far more non-Adventists at their work than anywhere else. Furthermore, their workmates see them on a long-term basis. They get acquainted with Adventists, see what Adventism is like, and see whether it makes a difference, whether it really works.

That is why the Lord calls most of us to work in the world, not to work full-time for the church. True, occasionally when someone finds the Lord he is also called into the ministry, but that is a rare thing. We must be careful not to confuse the two callings, and to remember that whether we work as a plumber, a teacher, a doctor, or a bus driver, that too is a calling from the Lord.

In New Testament teaching, every believer is a minister. The Lord doesn't call just a privileged few—He calls *all.*

Your Adventism will make a difference at work. Work situations are so diverse that I would be foolish to attempt a systematic listing of what you should or should not do. Instead, I will simply give a few illustrations of ways that make manifest the Adventist difference.

The World Bank, headquartered in Washington, D.C., is a large organization with many hundreds of employees. Quite a few are Adventists, drawn from a variety of ethnic backgrounds. For several years some of these Adventists at the World Bank have organized regular Bible studies during lunch breaks. With the approval of their bosses, they at times invite Adventist ministers to conduct studies. At other times they lead out themselves. They have seen some of their fellow workers choose Adventism as the result of these Bible studies. That is close to an ideal work situation—but one that you may not be able to duplicate.

My father worked for many years in the building trade. Although he had little education, although he rarely preached, his life touched many.

In his old age, when he had long since left off building

houses, I met people who remembered his work. One Sabbath when as a student home from college I preached in one of the Adelaide churches, a man came up to me. "You're the son of Joel Johnsson, aren't you?" he asked. "I want you to know that Joel had the reputation of being the hardest worker in the whole building industry."

I myself worked as an industrial chemist for three years before I answered the Lord's call to the gospel ministry. One day as I worked in the laboratory, I discovered that an older man whom I had seen from time to time knew my father. "Well!" he said. "I remember your father very well when I worked with him in the building trade. He'd never swear like the rest of us. He'd always bow his head and say a little grace before eating his lunch. He always brought a couple of Weetbix [made in Australia by our church-owned Sanitarium Health Food Company] for lunch. We all respected him because he worked so hard!"

Integrity, faithfulness, and hard work are qualities that men and women quickly notice and don't soon forget. In the long run, they are the finest witness for Adventism.

What if you work at a profession? The same qualities will set you apart and bring honor to your Lord.

Milton Murray, who is highly regarded in both church and nonchurch circles for his professionalism in philanthropic services, and his son Keith give the following 10 suggestions:

1. Strive for quality professional performance.
2. Be active in professional circles.
3. Join a service organization.
4. Volunteer leadership and time.
5. Initiate funding for a worthy cause.
6. Introduce your church pastor or leader to community VIPs (or vice versa).
7. Write letters to editors.
8. Share material you have found inspirational and helpful.

9. See others as sons and daughters of God.
10. Be sensitive to the problems of others.

(See "Ten Ways to Witness From Your Office," by Milton Murray and Keith B. Murray, *Adventist Review*, Mar. 5, 1987.)

Marilyn works as a secretary in an office of 200 people—and she's the only Adventist. How does she relate to the situation?

"I find myself daring to be different," she says. "My diet is different. My speech is different. Everything is different. It seems 'they' are on one side, I on the other.

"Yet I must try to make Christianity attractive and enjoyable. I never scorn the beliefs of other people—they are important to them. I compliment and encourage them in anything they do in their church or in their church attendance.

"If they have relatives or friends who are sick, I ask if they want our church to have special prayer for them. That always touches hearts. If they so desire, I pray with them right where they are.

"They watch everything I do. Every time my temper flares or I snap at someone, they see it. If I smile at an off-color joke, they see that. Although I stopped drinking cola drinks several years ago, they still come at times and check the contents of my paper cup to see if it's 7-Up in there or cola!

"The only time I talk about religion other than when asked is when someone mentions 'hell,' or burning forever. I tell them this isn't so, that it's a cruel satanic doctrine that has caused many to become atheists.

"I am the only Bible many of these people may read or see, the only Christian they will ever meet. I am honored that God thinks enough of me to put me in a position where I can be a daily witness to more than 200 people. It's a challenge. It's very difficult when your life has to *be* the sermon. But it's fun."

At Play

What about social functions at work? Birthday parties, Christmas celebrations, going-away parties—the liquor flows freely, the noise level rises, people get tipsy, and the Adventist feels like the proverbial fish out of water. Should we have anything to do with such occasions?

Adventists continually face situations like these. Your neighbors who aren't members of the church invite you to a wedding. You know the food and drink will not be "kosher"! Should you search around for an excuse not to go, or simply decline? Is this your opportunity to give them a sermonette on the evils of drink?

I remember well the Christmas parties in the chemical industry where I worked for several years—the entertainment, the singing, the jokes, and the drinking (especially the drinking, since some of my workmates had vowed to get stone drunk). I certainly didn't look forward to those occasions each year. Nonetheless, I used to put in an appearance simply to show myself friendly. I'd always leave early, just when things were getting lively.

Likewise in my doctoral studies. The students in biblical studies had organized themselves into sort of a club that met regularly once a week to discuss serious matters and about once a month for a party. The latter always involved drinking, usually plenty of it.

Noelene and I didn't relish going to these occasions, but from time to time we made the effort. Although we were not interested in many of the food items, we always found sufficient to munch on as we made polite conversation. Nor did anyone attempt to pressure us to join in the drinking. They provided nonalcoholic drinks for us. Usually we left after about an hour—the first to be on the road. In a sense it was only a token attendance, but nonetheless it showed that we cared enough to make the effort.

We were working for the church in India at the time, and I did my doctoral studies on an extended furlough. We left

Nashville for India just one week after my oral defense of the dissertation. The last Sunday evening some Adventist friends invited us around for supper. We walked in the door and—surprise! There were all my friends from the doctoral program, the major professor included. We had a lovely last evening together in an Adventist setting—no need to worry about inebriated drivers from that party!

Weddings, parties, social functions—where possible, I suggest that the Adventist say yes. The New Testament plainly teaches that Jesus was a sociable being. He was one of the most popular dinner guests in Jerusalem. Everyone, it seemed, from religious leaders to the despised tax collectors wanted Him to dine with them. He was so popular that His enemies accused Him of being a glutton and a winebibber! Ellen White tells us that Jesus made a special effort to be sociable, but that He was social to save *(The Desire of Ages,* pp. 150-151).

Nevertheless, at times sincere Adventists will find themselves isolated. At times you will be the only one in the group who doesn't eat or doesn't drink or doesn't go or who doesn't say yes.

What is the best way to say no?

Our daughter Julie recently completed a graduate degree in journalism at Northwestern University in Evanston, Illinois. Students in the program frequently got together to talk shop. They served alcoholic drinks. On these occasions and as she attended press conferences and seminars where everybody seemed to take alcoholic drinks, she quickly learned ways of saying no. On one occasion a friend said to her, "What! You don't drink? I've never met a journalist who didn't drink!"

It's OK not to drink in the eighties, Julie says. Just because you don't drink, you don't have to be a social leper.

Here are Julie's suggestions on ways to say no:

- **Don't apologize or try to hide your stand.**

Be up front. When you're invited to a party or dinner, say

beforehand, "Hey, I don't drink. Will that be a problem?"

● **At a restaurant mention only what you want to order.**

Ask for Perrier, if you like it, a soda drink, or fruit juice. There's no need to explain your order.

● **If you act hesitant or seem overly defensive, people may try to pressure you to enjoy a drink.**

So be firm but relaxed. Expect people to respect your decision.

● **Be prepared to explain your stand.**

Over dinner, someone is sure to ask why you choose not to drink. Here are some good responses:

1. "I prefer to be in control."
2. "As a Christian, I believe my body is the temple of God. I feel an obligation to remain sober."
3. "When I see the harm that drunks do, I don't want to support the alcohol industry in any way."
4. "I'm scared to drink. I have a relative who's an alcoholic."

Don't give an answer you don't believe. No need to preach a sermon. Give short, concise answers when questioned.

● **If alcohol has been a problem for you in the past, you may be wise not to party at all with the old gang.**

Work, study, play—Adventism need not lead to a diminished or shriveled life. A person doesn't need alcohol to make interesting conversation. If one is secure in oneself, one doesn't need liquor to boost confidence. More people are beginning to recognize that and come to admire men and women who can say no gracefully.

Of course, some people will see our distinctives as a barrier we have thrown up between them and us. So we need to take the initiative, break down the barrier by meeting them at the basic human level of friendliness and sociability.

That, it seems to me, is following in the footsteps of Jesus.

6

The Folks Next Door

Karen, a bubbly young Adventist, had recently moved. In an effort to get acquainted with her neighbors, she hit upon a plan. Visiting the apartments on her block, she would say, "Hi, I'm Karen. I've just moved into the neighborhood and would like to invite you over on Friday evening for a get-together. I'm not very good at singing and need people to help me sing and play the guitar."

She found several people who played the guitar, but not at a level where they'd be asked to perform in public. They were glad for the invitation.

The Friday night group at Karen's home soon became a favorite for many of her neighbors. They played and sang. Karen would fix a light vegetarian meal. "I didn't tell them it was vegetarian until they asked," she reports. Karen formed close friendships with several in the group.

One of her neighbors was having problems with her husband. Depressed, she didn't want to eat. Karen didn't get involved in the marital situation, but, on learning that her neighbor liked to walk, went on long walks with her. They'd start at 5:00 a.m. and would spend hours walking and talking. Gradually the depression lifted.

"Just being *there* for your neighbors when something happens—that's what counts," Karen says. "No need to press. They ask; they want to know. That's the best way to evangelize people.

"Very rarely do I start with the Bible. Instead, I try to live the principles and be available to my neighbors whenever they need me."

Karen's efforts have borne fruit. So far eight of her neighbors have been baptized.

But suppose you aren't the outgoing type—you simply couldn't pull off Karen's plan. What might you do?

Sam Monnier, associate director in the Church Ministries Department of the General Conference, has made a special study of how Adventists can relate positively to their neighbors. He notes:

"Our neighbors soon form an opinion about us from the way we act, work around the house, and treat members of our family. If I get angry when my son does not come home at a specified time, the neighbors soon know. They will discover whether ours is a happy home or whether we are just one more cluster of people living together.

"They may not seem to be watching us, and in all probability they are not, but they notice. They observe minute details, whether we bring flowers home on Friday afternoons, walk hand in hand with our spouse, open the car door gently for elderly people, and other similar gestures. They will read our facial expressions when we speak to each other. It's easy for them to detect what type of people we are.

"It isn't difficult to win the confidence of our neighbors if we live clean, happy Christian lives, talk kindly with them over the fence, inquire about their family, associate with their children and pets, and give them a helping hand.

"All these people around us are candidates for heaven. Our way of living should attract them. Soon they will tell their friends, 'The Monniers, our new neighbors, are Seventh-day Adventists. Every Saturday morning around nine o'clock the whole family, dressed in their best and with Bible in hand, head toward the church.' "

But is it enough simply to be a good influence? Since God loves our neighbors and we are His instruments on earth, His intermediaries, we must do something more than merely living a kind, exemplary life.

A Meal Together

Suppose Sam and Yvonne Monnier call a family council and agree to invite neighbors over for supper. Whom should they invite first? Their son suggests a family with children his age. Mrs. Monnier's choice will be the family of a neighbor lady with whom she spoke two or three times at the supermarket. Elder Monnier's choice will be the family of a gentleman with whom he chats about work, gardening, and the community. So husband, wife, and son talk it over. They agree to vote by secret ballot. After all, Switzerland, their country, is a very old and democratic land!

"One evening when the chosen neighbor is at home, my son and I go over to invite him and his family to our home," says Elder Monnier. "We say that we want to get acquainted with them and have them enjoy a special Swiss menu. The answer is usually yes. Generally no one refuses an invitation for a meal. Besides, the way we present our invitation encourages a positive response.

"The first visit is important," Monnier says. "It can be the beginning of a friendly relationship." The Monniers pray much about this first contact. Their one purpose is to lead these neighbors to Jesus.

When the guests arrive, they possibly notice the Bible on the coffee table. The Monniers chat for a few minutes on general topics—the weather, families, work. Soon they invite the guests to the table. Now comes their *first testimony*. The host says, "We are so happy to have you in our home today. We are Christians. We'd like to ask God's blessing on the food before we eat. It's our family custom to allow my wife to invite one of us to offer grace." At this point Yvonne responds, usually calling upon the youngest member of her family to offer prayer.

"The prayer usually impresses our guests," Sam continues, "because we've spent several days in spiritual preparation for this visit. We prayed frequently, asking God for the wisdom to deal with our guests."

Typically the child's prayer goes something like this: "Dear Lord, thank You for our new friends. You know how much we care for them already. Thank You for the food You provide for us. Bless our families. Please bless every child in the world. In Jesus' name, amen."

Many who have experienced the Monniers' hospitality later confide that what impressed them most during their first visit was "your child's prayer before the meal."

The Monniers serve an excellent fruit juice as their *second testimony*. "With a French name like ours, people expect us to serve red or white wine," Sam says. "I explain that as a 14-year-old, I saw the evils of alcohol and decided never to drink a drop of it. I determined later to marry a Christian with the same commitment and raise children alcohol-free. 'But we have a lovely fruit punch to offer you.' People usually react by admitting that they don't drink either, except for special occasions."

Toward the end of the meal comes the *third testimony*. Usually someone asks what kind of meat was served. This allows Sam the opportunity to comment on vegetarianism. He links the family's dietary preference to Bible reading. Sam explains how he discovered that the perfect diet, which God gave Adam and Eve, consisted of fruits and grains. People who followed this diet were strong, tall, and very healthy. They lived more than 900 years. After the Flood, people had to eat animals. Even then they ate the flesh of only certain "clean" animals. "If today we are able to put together a good, balanced diet without incorporating meat into it, why not do so?" Sam concludes. "The Bible doesn't prohibit meat, but shouldn't we always try to eat the best?"

Sam is quick to point out that in mentioning their stand against alcoholic beverages and their choice of the best diet, they separate these decisions from any requirement of the church. "A well-balanced individual wants to refrain from injuring his body and can reach these decisions independently from church teachings," he adds.

After concluding the meal with a delicious dessert, the Monniers visit further in the living room while the children play in the basement. Sam and Yvonne give their neighbors a chance to talk.

When the guests are about to leave, Sam tells them how he came to choose to follow Jesus. "It's more effective to be a good listener, but in order to build confidence, also share something about yourself. Be a little vulnerable," Sam advises.

His *short testimony* touches on the blessings of enjoying a happy spiritual family. Although others may be able to tell a more dramatic experience of how they lived in the world and how God brought them into His service, the testimony of one reared in a Christian home can be equally effective, Sam thinks.

After such a testimony, the neighbors may ask a few questions or want some details. "Do not challenge anyone or expound on doctrines," Sam advises. "Just tell what happened in *your life,* and then conclude by reading a promise from the Bible. This should not last more than 15 seconds and should be followed by prayer.

"Keep the prayer brief and personal. Thank God for the privilege of meeting neighbors, for the company they provide, and for the opportunity of sharing experiences. Pray for any problems your new friends may be facing. If members of their family are sick, mention them. If they are having professional difficulties or educational problems, present them to God. Thank God for the privilege of reading His Word and praying together." At the end Sam asks God to "Give us another chance to meet, to get better acquainted, and to help one another." Such prayers have touched many.

This first visit follows the pattern of the early Christians, who were breaking bread in the homes every day. How successful they were in winning souls!

What will the next step be? The neighbors will probably extend a return invitation. Of course, they will face the problem of preparing a vegetarian meal. If the wife mentions this to Yvonne, she will invite her over. Preparing a vegetarian dish together in the Monniers' kitchen will provide another opportunity to get even better acquainted. Before they separate, Yvonne will offer a short prayer.

Build Solid Friendships

Our neighbors' doors will not remain closed if we show tact, discretion, and friendliness. The secret is to know how to act with them. We must not be hasty. Only when a solid friendship has been built can we lead them in a systematic study of God's Word. Because they have learned to trust us, they will listen.

Of course, not every neighbor will become a Seventh-day Adventist. Everyone, however, will remember and treasure our friendship. Prejudice will be broken, and this is important in itself.

During the second visit our neighbors may have a few questions to ask. Before leaving them, we should never forget to read a well-chosen Bible promise and pray together. Decide with the members of your family what text would be the most appropriate for the circumstances. Involve your children. Teach them early to love others and to share with them.

On New Year's morning Sam Monnier takes each of his neighbors some of his wife's pastries with a book such as *Steps to Christ* or *The Great Controversy*. They have a wonderful relationship with their neighbors. Many of them are involved in their own church activities, but their doors are open wide to the Monniers.

"One sunny afternoon our son called us at the office," Sam recalls. "A police officer had entered our house through an open window. He left a message on the table to pick up our house key at the police station.

"Astonished, I went to the police station. The kind officer greeted me with a smile and handed over the key. Puzzled, I said, 'I need a word of explanation. Why did you enter my house through a window? How did you know the window was open? Is this common procedure?'

" 'Oh,' he said, 'don't you know? This morning your neighbor lady called us, saying, "Please hurry. The Monniers are very careful people. I have never seen their windows left open. There must be a thief in their house. Hurry!" So we went with three police cars, circled the block, and I entered your house through the open window. Everything was in order; there was no sign of any burglar around. So I took your key and left the note. Please, don't leave your keys, even inside the door.'

"I felt relieved. The police officer continued, 'Say, who are you? Why were your neighbors so anxious for us to protect your house? People aren't usually so friendly in Washington.'

"With immense satisfaction, I told him that I was a Seventh-day Adventist minister. 'Oh,' he said, 'I know of your church. There are many Seventh-day Adventists around here.' I told him that I regularly visit my neighbors. Before I left his office, I asked him about his family and offered a short prayer. As soon as I said 'amen,' he asked, 'Do you ever pray with your neighbors?'

" 'Oh, yes, every time we meet.'

" 'Well,' he said, 'that's the answer. Now I understand why this lady was so anxious to protect your house.'

"The friendly ties we had established in our neighborhood were a real blessing in this unexpected way.

"What a privilege it should be to pray when we visit! Once as I left my neighbor's home without offering a word of prayer, the lady immediately requested, 'Sir, please pray with me. I always look forward to these quiet moments when you pray with us in our home.'

"We began our invitations by choosing the neighbor my

son preferred. A few days later we invited the neighbor my wife chose. Next came the neighbor I had in mind. Following this pattern, we invited as many neighbor families as possible. The more we got acquainted, the more effective was our witnessing.

"Recently one of our lay evangelists from Minnesota remarked, 'Elder Monnier, we are very friendly with our next-door neighbor. We invited him to our place and then we went over to his home. We have been very good friends for several years. But nothing has happened.'

" 'Why concentrate on only one neighbor?' I said. 'Why don't you invite other neighbors, perhaps one every month or every three months? That way, you contact from 4 to 12 families every year. The chances of reaching someone are very real.' It is a matter of simple mathematics. Because one neighbor is not responding, why conclude that this method is a failure?

"In speaking of meals, I do not have a banquet in mind. Prepare a simple meal. Our wives are busy and often tired. The meal itself is not the most important factor; getting acquainted with our neighbors is what counts. Our budgets will permit a simple get-together once a month or once a quarter. Have everyone in the family help your wife prepare a good meal. This may be her successful Bible study.

"Are our finances lower than those of the early Christians? Remember that one of the secrets of their success was that every day in their homes they shared food with others. They broke bread together (Acts 2:42, 46).

"In this way, early Christians had ample time to share their testimonies, speak about Jesus, and lead people to the foot of His cross. Can we not do the same? As God's remnant people we can use a simple biblical method to establish contact with others. This was one reason why early Christians won converts among the inhabitants of Jerusalem. The priests complained, 'Ye have filled Jerusalem with your doctrine' (Acts 5:28).

THE FOLKS NEXT DOOR

"If it worked then, it will work now. A meal together builds friendships faster, and for Christ, more souls won!"*

---

*Adapted from S. F. Monnier, "Reaching Out to Neighbors," *Adventist Review,* May 26, 1983.

7

Fitting Into Your Church Family

Just as a newlywed finds that he has married into a family, so the one who chooses Adventism sooner or later discovers that he or she has acquired a world family. The experience may not be without some trauma, but it also provides rich possibilities for developing a support system and genuine friends. In fact, some church friends in time may grow closer than family. It's largely up to you.

This chapter will give you ideas on how to fit in with your new church family. You will learn how to cultivate new friendships, how to respond if you find yourself left out, how to deal with problems of rearing your children, how to keep the Sabbath, how to shop, and how to assume responsibilities in the family.

Cultivating New Friendships

The fact that Nora has changed religions makes no difference in her attitude toward her family and friends. "I love you just as much as before," she assures her close friend Pat. But Pat isn't so sure. She already has lost a bridge partner and finds Nora unable or unwilling—she isn't sure which—to join in the Friday night activities that they had previously enjoyed.

Nora has two options. Because she cannot return to her

former pattern of living, she can either gradually withdraw from the friendship with Pat and seek other Adventist friends, or she can go out of her way to establish new outlets for their friendship and seek to link Pat to the new network of Adventist social life.

Because she genuinely loves Pat and values her friendship, Nora chooses the second option. After her baptism Nora reassures Pat that she is happy in her new commitment and that conversion to Adventism has made her a better person and not the warped woman that Pat fears.

So Nora takes every opportunity to contact Pat and keep the lines of communication open. If Pat reacts suspiciously to invitations to a musical program at the church, Nora suggests a symphony concert or a shopping expedition instead.

If being with Pat weakens Nora's commitment to healthful living or spiritual things, Nora may decide to let the friendship lapse. But if the friendship proves wholesome and helpful, she will naturally pursue it.

Sometimes the Noras who join the church discover themselves rejected by family and friends. In this case they will find encouragement in establishing social ties with their new Adventist family.

But as with any family, we must accept a measure of good and indifferent experiences. Some well-adjusted church members threaten the self-concept of unsure newcomers. Others endlessly offer unwanted advice. But here and there, in the most unexpected places, we find just the right person to boost our morale and add a sparkle to life.

Some suggestions to guide you in establishing new relationships within the family include the following:

● **Look for friends who fit in with your family.**

The ideal, of course, is another family that likes to do things with your family. Sometimes one parent may find a congenial soul who fits in like an indulgent aunt or uncle and is accepted by all family members.

● **Friendships should complement family relationships.**

A friendship that threatens family relationships—if a spouse reacts negatively to the friend, for instance—must be left to flourish at church and not be allowed to spill over into family life, where it will cause dissension.

● **Retain your own individuality in a friendship.**

New members need not defer to the opinions of Adventist friends on the assumption that the latter have been in the way longer and are therefore wiser. On the contrary, people for whom Christian living has become habitual may have forgotten the reasons for their way of life—the very reasons that are yet fresh and vital in the thinking of the newcomer.

● **Allow your fresh approach to religion and living to guide you in social interaction.**

Your commitment to Jesus may prove a blessing to members of the church family, just as it does to your friends outside the church. For instance, don't be afraid to discuss what Jesus means to you. Encourage others to share with you their own particular spiritual insights. Accept their views, but don't feel obliged to change yours to conform with theirs.

● **Feel secure in your social status.**

Often new Adventists get a shock when they go to church. They find it the best-dressed gathering in town! Adventists try to look their best for church and so in general are more careful about their appearance at worship than other Christians (that lovely suit or dress may be the only good one a believer owns, however).

So be yourself. Adventism isn't a social club. You are welcome regardless of how well you dress.

Incidentally, Adventism lifts people socially. Its principles do lead to better health and more comfortable living. As we tithe and give generously, the Lord surely blesses us.

When Your Efforts Fail

What if your efforts to mingle and belong in the family leave you still on the outside? What if your children feel like outcasts? What do you do to win acceptance? Churches are more like hospitals for the sick than country clubs for the healthy. If you encounter a congregation that believes themselves to be the latter, fellowship may seem only a distant possibility.

Before the Smith family joined the church, they had gone through a long bout of difficult times. The children's clothes, gleaned from a Goodwill store, proclaimed the difference between them and the other children. The other Adventist children had attended the same church school since kindergarten. But though they wanted to make Debbie and Jay Smith feel welcome, most of the children hadn't developed social skills to the point of reaching out to strangers. They simply sat and stared.

Debbie saved the day. Her naturally bubbly nature broke down the initial shyness of the Sabbath school class. The social skills she had developed in a large public school helped her weather the initially cold reception of the others. The Smiths, encouraged by Debbie's success in making friends, never wavered in their attitude of goodwill toward the church. In time they were integrated into the family.

But sometimes things simply don't work out as happily as they did for the Smiths. What should newcomers do then?

Whatever you do, don't give up! The kingdom of God is worth waiting for. Find out where the next nearest congregation meets. It may be worth driving 30 minutes to worship with a church family that makes you feel at home. Look for another family or a single person who seems lonely. Start your own circle of caring so that others will find in your church what you missed. Invite someone to Sabbath lunch. Thank a young person for his part in the service.

Chances are you won't be able to take the church by storm. Begin quietly to reach out and make friends. Ask a question; seek help. Later you can offer help when a work bee is called or a member is discouraged.

Whether integration is fast or slow, stressful or painless, try to maintain an optimistic but realistic view of the church family. Most Adventists would agree that their fellow church members are supportive, caring people. But nobody would go so far as to describe them as perfect. For no matter how much we grow in grace, we all must still admit to weaknesses. (The occasional person who claims perfection also usually proves extremely tiresome.)

And while the church provides shelter against opposition and rest for those weary of sin, we cannot count on the church to solve all our problems. Christians must be prepared to work out their own salvation with fear and trembling (Philippians 2:12, 13). Ultimately we stand before God as individuals.

Rearing Your Child

The church is a place to take children to worship God and where parents receive encouragement through association with other godly parents. But childrearing is first the duty of parents. Parents shouldn't expect the church to assume their responsibility in this respect. Parents must be just as aware of what is going on when their children are at church as they are when at home.

We must accept the responsibility to teach our children godliness. Godlikeness isn't achieved through contact on one day per week but is nurtured every day.

Problems may arise when your children cite the practice of other families in the church or church school to support their behavior. Parents must quietly, lovingly point out children's responsibility to God. They should encourage children to serve God willingly and cheerfully, daring to do differently if necessary. Drifting with the current can be dangerous—even if the current is the Adventist mainstream. If we want our children to stay Adventist, even after they leave the nest, we must encourage them to renew that choice on a daily basis.

I hope you can afford to send your children to an Adventist school. Our schools aren't perfect, but they give the

Christian option a chance to be heard. They're the best place for our children to be.

If, however, because of finances, disagreement with your non-SDA spouse, or some other reason you are unable to send your children to an Adventist school, don't feel bad about yourself. You aren't a second-class member, nor are your children any less valuable or loved in the church family. Make that very clear to your children—although they aren't at school with their Adventist friends, they can still feel good about themselves.

Let me tell you about Cindy, though—unlike most of the people I refer to in this book—I wish her story ended differently.

Cindy was a single parent with two children in public school. Her children led her to join the church—they enjoyed Vacation Bible School. Cindy was excited when she discovered Christianity and the Adventist Christian lifestyle.

As Cindy began to make friends among the church family, she learned that others her age sent their children to church school. They told her how wonderful the school was. Cindy began to think, *If I don't send my children to church school, I'll deprive them of their salvation.*

So she placed the children in an Adventist school—even though she couldn't meet the bills on her income as a secretary. Before long her account ran into thousands of dollars. Because she couldn't pay, she had to put her youngsters in public school again.

But the local church came to her aid and settled the account. Cindy took the children out of public school and placed them in another church school.

Once again, however, the bill ran up. Embarrassed, Cindy once again placed the children in public school. Guilt-ridden and despairing, heavily in debt, she left the church. If only someone had thought to reassure Cindy that whether or not her children were in church school, they would all be valued by their Adventist friends.

Adventist education is the best investment you can make. If you can afford to send your child to an Adventist school, do so! It's better to give up some material possessions for a while (Noelene and I went without a piano for seven years during the peak expense years of educating our children) in order to give them the opportunity of learning in a Christian environment.

How to Keep the Sabbath

The deacon was just opening up the church when Bruce drove up on his first Sabbath really excited about Adventism.

He loved studying the Bible in the Sabbath school class. Then the anticipation of the 11 o'clock worship hour, joining in the singing, praying, and listening to the pastor's sermon—how his spirits soared.

After the service Bruce shook a few hands and waited around. Members were driving away; the deacon began to lock up. Bruce went home.

That Sabbath afternoon was "dead time," as he described it to us. Wanting to guard the Sabbath jealously, he went to bed and stayed there, just reading and sleeping.

As Bruce studied and grew in Adventism, he was embarrassed to learn that sleeping isn't exactly the meaning of "resting" on the Sabbath day! He wouldn't think of sleeping on the job during his regular workdays—why should he treat God's holy day like that? And he wasn't impressed by the jokes of longtime church members about "lay activities" for Sabbath afternoons. He wanted to honor the Sabbath.

No one had instructed Bruce in how to keep the Sabbath. However, his studies of the Bible and Ellen White's writings led him to chart his own course. He began to invite a small group of friends home for Sabbath lunch. After they'd eaten a simple meal, they spent most of the afternoon studying a topic of common interest or discussing some aspect of practical Christianity. Later he discovered other activities that fulfilled him—visiting a nursing home, taking walks in a quiet park, calling on a friend.

How to Shop

Even people who have prided themselves on being intelligent shoppers will discover new shopping skills after they choose Adventism. Two types of shopping particularly demand attention—shopping for food and for clothing.

Joan's realization that a change in shopping habits was needed came as the result of a shock. "It blew my mind," she says. "I had just cooked chicken with lard when my pastor happened to say that lard isn't good for us." Remembering to read labels to determine the types of fats used in products was a new skill for Joan. But as she became adept at this, it no longer took so much time and attention that going grocery shopping was a loathsome chore.

Some facts she learned with the help of Adventist friends include:

● **Vegetable fats are usually more healthful than animal fats.**

But a highly saturated fat such as coconut oil can be as dangerous as lard when it comes to raising blood cholesterol, even though it contains no cholesterol itself.

● **Soft margarine in tubs is less saturated than stick margarine.**

However, even the best margarines and vegetable oils should be used sparingly. Thus you won't want to make a habit of eating fried foods and pastries.

● **Sugar should be avoided, especially in foods that aren't even desserts.**

Labels list the ingredients of a product in order of quantity. When cereals, for instance, list sugar before the grain, they have more sugar than cereal! Health-conscious Adventists try to bake their own desserts so that they can cut down on the sugar content. A good rule of thumb is to halve the sugar called for in most recipes.

● **You may want to avoid foods with preservatives added.**

Many health-conscious individuals try to avoid ingesting the many chemicals used in prepared foods to retard spoilage. Responding to this concern, some cereal manufacturers add BHP, a preservative, to the packaging rather than to the food.

● **Check the calorie content of products.**

Even if you aren't into counting calories and are thin as a rail, check the calorie count on labels. For instance, granola bars with the lowest calorie count probably have the least sugar and fat.

● **Try to use more legumes in your diet.**

Complex carbohydrates used with foods such as dried beans and peas help replace meat proteins and are an excellent alternative. Soybeans are best, but variety is always important. Mexican foods—burritos, tacos, or chili beans—provide tasty ways of fixing red beans. What about the undesirable aftereffect from beans? A tablespoon of lemon juice added to the beans seems to remove the problem for many people. Beans are not only good for you; they save money too, especially if you buy them dry and cook them yourself. A pressure cooker is especially helpful when cooking soybeans. Be sure to follow safety instructions that come with the pressure cooker. Most other beans cook well in a slow cooker (for example, a Crockpot) or on top of the stove.

● **Use whole grains, fruits, and vegetables.**

Stone-ground whole wheat flour is the best because all the nutrients and fiber of the grain have been retained, but it is not always practical for everyone all the time. Eating an orange is healthier in the long run than drinking orange juice, because your body needs the roughage and the unidentified nutrients that have been strained out of the juice. Similarly, eat fruits without peeling them whenever the peel is edible (obviously, you don't want to eat banana skins!), and boil potatoes in their skins. Peel the potato after it is cooked if you cannot eat the peel. Basic principle: eat all food as close to the way they were grown as possible.

● **Hot seasonings and spices may irritate your stomach.**

Nonetheless, food doesn't have to taste bland and flavorless if you use fruits and vegetables that are as fresh as possible (never stint on freshness) and are cooked quickly in a small amount of water and are seasoned with healthful herbs. It's probably easiest to remember to avoid red or black pepper and anything that burns the mouth (except onions). Such spices as cloves, cinnamon, nutmeg, cardamom, and ginger have the potential to irritate the stomach, so use sparingly.

● **Nonmeat eaters must balance their diets with vegetable proteins.**

Foods that are considered complex carbohydrates (grains, cereals, pastas, and legumes) also contain protein and are great substitutes for meat. But vegetable proteins aren't complete in themselves. Peanut butter sandwiches, for instance, combine nuts and grains to make a complete protein. Some other good vegetable protein combinations are wheat-gluten products (such as Stakelets), with leafy greens, legumes, or nuts; and bread and cereal with milk. Be wary about eliminating milk from the diet. It is *the* major source of calcium.

● **Health consciousness has its own rewards.**

To fully enjoy the benefits of the Adventist lifestyle, you should get some recipe books and read up on nutrition. Your local Adventist Book Center has available a variety of nutrition and recipe books. Generally, the more you put into life, the more benefit you receive. The more healthfully you eat, the better you feel and the longer you are likely to live a fulfilling life. But as with all good things, you can go to extremes. It could be better to eat a little meat than to follow vegetarianism grudgingly or without compensating properly for the lack of meat. Also, beware of the many inadequately qualified people who write authoritative-sounding books on nutrition that appear in otherwise-legitimate book and health food stores. Check with a registered dietitian at any hospital to help you determine the credentials of such an author. Even a non-Adventist dietitian should be able to advise you appropriately. And because things taste bad doesn't mean that they are better for you! Healthful living tastes good.

Shopping for clothing is not as complicated as shopping for food. But you will look purchases over in a way that you didn't have to before. Because you have a new attitude toward money—since you return to the Lord His portion—you will find yourself taking the extra effort to look for bargains. You will also look critically before purchasing to decide if the item conforms to your new awareness of simplicity and modesty.

Women begin looking more closely at the design of clothing. Where they once dressed up low necklines with jewelry, they now choose styles and fabrics that look good plain. And considering what a jeweled buckle has added to the price of a dress, you will prefer to select something else rather than cut off the buckle.

A hint that Noelene's mother passed on to her when shopping is still sound advice: choose colors and styles that best enhance your personality. If you tone up or down the colors of your clothing, you won't need to add all that color to your lips and cheeks. And people will more easily notice the love of Jesus radiating from your eyes.

Assuming Responsibilities

The Adventist family is a great family to belong to. But we cannot rely on the family to carry us through to the kingdom. Family members must accept certain responsibilities that go with fellowship.

● **Each Adventist family member should accept at least one responsibility connected with the church.**

If you are not elected to a church office, you may help by being prepared each Sabbath to invite a visitor or elderly member home to lunch. Or you may ask the pastor to provide names of people for you to visit.

● **Choose at least one project that will make you useful to the community at large.**

Join a service organization in the community, volunteer at a hospital, or take it upon yourself to visit your neighbors and share a church paper or book with them. Take your children with you so that they will learn to be useful church members.

● **Take an interest in the world at large.**

Read about other countries, pray for missions, give for missions. For an exciting sense of involvement, take up a Sabbath school Investment partnership. Choosing a project whereby you can make a little extra money for missions is called Investment. If your church doesn't feature it in Sabbath school, ask your minister about it.

● **Arrive on time for worship services.**

This is one of the most helpful ways you can serve your church.

● **Invite a neighbor to services.**

Not only does this build goodwill in your community, but it motivates other church members to prepare better services and share their faith.

As a new church member, you have access to a wonderful body of possibilities. What the church comes to mean in your life, however, could largely be up to you. Embrace the possibilities, welcome the opportunities, and enjoy the blessings that will follow.

8

After the Euphoria

Many people enter the Seventh-day Adventist Church riding a spiritual and emotional high. They feel clean. They have been made new. They have found a church that earnestly tries to follow the teachings of the Bible.

But the realities of living as an Adventist on a daily basis sometimes bring them down to earth with a thud. They find that the church where they now worship Sabbath by Sabbath is quite a bit different from the church of the evangelistic meetings.

They chose Adventism in a large hall where hundreds of people came out nightly to study the Bible together. But they discover that the local Adventist church is a small, unpretentious building, with many of the members aged and most of them women. The evangelist spoke powerfully, illustrating his addresses with slides and other visual materials. But the preaching at the local Adventist church, although sincere, may well be mediocre, and is often done by the church elder. They miss the lively singing and the musical solos of the evangelistic series.

They feel let down in other areas. "When we joined the Adventist Church, the thing that disappointed us most was the conduct of many of the church members," said Allen and Betty. "We found that many of them simply didn't practice the beliefs of the church."

For these and other reasons, new Adventists may find that

the spiritual and emotional high of entry into the church often vanishes like the morning mist that burns off in the rising sun. How do we cope when the euphoria is gone?

● **Remember that faith is different from feeling.**

For several years I oversaw the boys in a boarding academy. One evening as I was going from room to room in the dormitory, I found Ron in a troubled state of mind. After a while he began to tell me why.

"I think I've committed the unpardonable sin, Mr. Johnsson," he confided. "When I pray, God doesn't hear my prayer. I get up from my knees feeling no different from when I started praying. My prayers just bounce back to me from the ceiling. God must have cast me off, or I wouldn't feel this way."

"Oh, no, He hasn't!" I answered. "Ron, the very fact that you feel concerned about spiritual things shows that you haven't committed the unpardonable sin. As I understand the Scriptures, the hallmark of that sin is that a person is careless—he doesn't care about God or what happens to him eternally. I can tell without a shadow of a doubt that you have not committed the unpardonable sin."

"Then why don't I feel as though God hears me?" Ron responded. "If God loves me and is interested in me, surely I ought to feel it when I pray."

"Ron," I replied, "God nowhere promises us that we'll always feel close to Him. Faith isn't feeling. Faith is trusting Him, believing His Word, whether or not He sends us an emotional high. At times He does give us a good feeling, but not always. He wants us to keep on following Him, regardless of how we feel."

Many new Christians fall into the same trap. When the initial euphoria goes, they begin to think they have lost their Christian experience, or begin to doubt that what they had experienced was real. They may question whether they made the right decision in choosing Adventism.

Ours is an age that places great store by feelings—too

much store. The message in popular songs, movies, and television programs is: "If it feels right, it is right." Over and over, advertisers play on our feelings in an attempt to get us to buy their products.

Now, feelings aren't bad—after all, they came from God, who made us. But feelings are deceptive. We get up one morning feeling great, but on the way to work someone says, "Bill, are you OK? You look *terrible!*" What happens? Immediately the day, which had seemed so bright and sunny, clouds over. All it takes is for someone else to make a similar remark, and we feel like quitting and going home!

When it comes to the Christian life, emotions can be downright misleading. The point is this: *we can feel great when actually we are far from the Lord, and we can feel down when actually we are close to Him.*

Look at Acts 9:1-3: "Meanwhile, Saul was still breathing out murderous threats against the Lord's disciples. He went to the high priest and asked him for letters to the synagogues in Damascus, so that if he found any there who belonged to the Way, whether men or women, he might take them as prisoners to Jerusalem. As he neared Damascus on his journey, suddenly a light from heaven flashed around him" (NIV).

Saul is a man on an emotional high. He is full of zeal for God, and feels great about it—but he certainly isn't doing God's will! Saul of Tarsus, not yet converted, is terrorizing Christians, going to any lengths to stamp them out.

Now look at Matthew 27:45, 46: "From the sixth hour until the ninth hour darkness came over all the land. About the ninth hour Jesus cried out in a loud voice, *'Eloi, Eloi, lama sabachthani?'*—which means, 'My God, my God, why have you forsaken me?'" (NIV). Here is a Man plumbing the depths of human tragedy. He feels utterly alone, forsaken by God.

Yet He is not alone! Jesus of Nazareth, our Saviour, is dying on the cross. He has become the sin-bearer, taking on

Himself the guilt of the universe. And all that He is suffering comes from the Father's will. That Father, who at this moment seems so distant, is, in fact, suffering with the Son as the Godhead makes possible our salvation.

For many years I taught religion and Bible. I liked to demonstrate the difference between faith and feeling like this: I would write on the chalkboard 2 + 2 = 4. Then I would ask the class, "How do you feel about that?" Some students would look startled at the question, others amused. One or two would grin and say, "Fine!" Then I would go on: "It doesn't matter how you feel about it; 2 + 2 = 4 and always will equal 4, whether you feel fine or whether you feel terrible. The statement 2 + 2 = 4 is a fact, not a feeling."

Now look at some of the great facts of the universe.

"If we confess our sins, he is faithful and just and will forgive us our sins and purify us from all unrighteousness" (1 John 1:9, NIV).

"For God so loved the world that he gave his one and only Son, that whoever believes in him shall not perish but have eternal life" (John 3:16, NIV).

"And we know that in all things God works for the good of those who love him, who have been called according to his purpose" (Romans 8:28, NIV).

"He who did not spare his own Son, but gave him up for us all—how will he not also, along with him, graciously give us all things?" (verse 32, NIV).

"But he said to me, 'My grace is sufficient for you, for my power is made perfect in weakness'" (2 Corinthians 12:9, NIV).

"The Lord is my shepherd, I shall lack nothing" (Psalm 23:1, NIV).

"But now, this is what the Lord says—he who created you, O Jacob, he who formed you, O Israel: 'Fear not, for I have redeemed you; I have called you by name; you are mine. When you pass through the waters, I will be with you; and when you pass through the rivers, they will not sweep over you. When you walk through the fire, you will not be burned; the flames will not set you ablaze' " (Isaiah 43:1, 2, NIV).

"To him who is able to keep you from falling and to present you before his glorious presence without fault and with great joy" (Jude 24, NIV).

These are just a few of the promises of God found in His Word. These promises aren't *ifs* or *perhaps's* or *maybes*—they are *facts*. Regardless of how we may feel at a particular time, we are simply to take these promises and live by them. For instance, if we confess our sins in Jesus' name, God *does* forgive us, regardless of how we feel. It's a fact—not a feeling.

● **Give all and take all—every day.**

For some time after I became a Christian, I struggled to please the Lord. It seemed comparatively easy to come to Jesus, but so much harder to live for Him. I had come to Jesus as a sinner, bowing at the foot of the cross, confessing my sins. I had risen in the assurance that He had heard me and forgiven me. I had been baptized, I had confessed Jesus as Saviour and Lord, and I had gone forth to walk in newness of life.

But now it seemed I was on my own. Now I was a child of the King—and He expected me to live like His child! When I let Him down—which was frequently—I felt terrible.

But then one day I discovered Colossians 2:6: "So then, just as you received Christ Jesus as Lord, continue to live in him" (NIV). There it was—the formula for daily Christian living, and just for me!

This text tells me that the way we *live* as a Christian is exactly the same way as we *become* a Christian. How did we become a Christian? By giving all and taking all. Giving our all to Jesus—all our sinfulness, all our doubts, all our fears. And by taking all—all His righteousness, all His forgiveness, all His love, all His strength.

We came to the cross, confessing our unworthiness, claiming no righteousness of our own. And day by day we are to live just like that—by His strength, not our own. We are to die and be reborn.

For me, that means starting the day right. I am a morning person. I like to get up early, and I work best in the morning. So because I am a child of the King, I give Him my best time. I try never to start the day without first spending time with Him, at least 20 minutes in the study of the Bible, as well as in communing with Him, telling Him all my hopes and fears, laying my day before Him.

You may not be a morning person. Your best time may be at night. Whenever that time is, give part of it to Jesus. Daily give yourself to Him, and take Him.

It's no harder to live as a Christian than to become a Christian—that's what Colossians 2:6 assures us. And I know from my own experience that like His other promises that Scripture is true.

● **Living by the Spirit.**

The Lord doesn't promise us that we will always feel emotionally high, but He promises never to leave us. "Never will I leave you; never will I forsake you" (Hebrews 13:5, NIV). "And surely I will be with you always, to the very end of the age" (Matthew 28:20, NIV).

Jesus is always with us through the presence of the Holy Spirit. The Spirit's nature is a mystery. He is invisible, and in a way we cannot fathom, present everywhere at the same time. He is not Jesus, but He is God, one of the three members of the Godhead. And He carries on the work of Jesus.

Paul tells us, "Those who are led by the Spirit of God are sons of God" (Romans 8:14, NIV). "If anyone does not have the Spirit of Christ, he does not belong to Christ" (verse 10, NIV).

Christianity is a transforming friendship. We have friends, and they influence us. The deepest and longest-lasting friendships—like those between husband and wife, or between parent and child—influence us greatly.

We cannot see Jesus, but He is alive. We can know Him as our best friend, walking with us day by day. He can be as real and close to us as any human friend. And that friendship will influence us, gradually transforming us into His likeness. "And we, who with unveiled faces all reflect the Lord's glory, are being transformed into his likeness with ever-increasing glory, which comes from the Lord, who is the Spirit" (2 Corinthians 3:18, NIV).

In any friendship, however, we have to take time to communicate. If in a marriage the husband and wife never bother to show little attentions, never take the time to share secrets and problems, don't write when they are separated, the marriage withers and dies. And if we don't take time to talk to Jesus, our best friend, and to listen to Him by reading the Bible, His love letter to us, our Christianity will wither and die also.

These things make no sense to the non-Christian. But for those who believe, those who live day by day by the Spirit, they make sense altogether. Again, let Paul have the last word: "I have been crucified with Christ and I no longer live, but Christ lives in me. The life I live in the body, I live by faith in the Son of God, who loved me and gave himself for me" (Galatians 2:19, 20, NIV).

● **What about church members who aren't living as they should?**

You are disappointed in them, and so is the Lord. But be patient.

Remember, the church isn't a club for the perfect. It's a hospital for sick people. You'll meet some lovely, wonderful Christians in the Seventh-day Adventist Church. Some will become the closest friends you have in this life. You'll find some others far less attractive, however. You'll wonder how they could be so mean, petty, judgmental, or downright hypocritical.

But the church is a hospital. When you're sick, the place to be is in a hospital, where you can get the best attention and make steady progress toward perfect health. And the fact is, we're all sick. Some of us are sicker than others. We don't all have the same sicknesses, but we all suffer from one terrible malady—sin.

So turn your eyes on Jesus, not on other people. The writer to the Hebrews advises us: "Fix [your] eyes on Jesus, the author and perfecter of our faith, who for the joy set before him endured the cross, scorning its shame, and sat down at the right hand of the throne of God" (Hebrews 12:2, NIV). Jesus is the only One who will never disappoint you, who will never fall short, who will never let you down.

The more you look to Him and His perfect righteousness, the more you'll realize how far short you fall of that ideal. And that will make you that much more tolerant and patient with your fellow church members, who also fall short of His glory but who are striving to be like Him.

After the euphoria—what then? Some peaks, some valleys—certainly not a life of unbroken emotional ecstasy. But a life of trusting in Jesus, of looking to Him, and of day by day growing more like Him.

And as the days come and go, your Adventist identity will be growing also. We'll take a closer look at this in the next chapter.

9

Developing an Adventist Identity

As an Anglican, Lettie McFarland had a strong sense of her church. Lettie was attracted to Adventist teachings through a series of public evangelistic meetings. And while she believed the truth that she heard and began to attend an Adventist church on Sabbath, she had no intention of ever leaving the high Church of England.

But the wooings of the Spirit changed all that. One Sabbath she chose to throw in her lot with the Adventists. However, for months after her baptism she still thought more as an Anglican than as an Adventist.

Val and Pam Harrison were 12 and 10, respectively, when they joined the Adventist Church. After meeting some Adventists their own age at church, they realized that they didn't quite fit in. Perhaps attending a church school would make a difference, so they urged their parents to enroll them in the fall. All through the summer they worked at trying to fit in with the Adventists, trying to think like them and contribute to their conversations.

Even when school started, the Harrison girls did not quite fit in at first. Why were they different? What could they do to feel more like the others? "Why don't you carefully watch what the others do and listen to what they say?" their mom suggested. "Maybe you'll pick it up. It takes time."

It does take time to develop a sense of what it means to be a Seventh-day Adventist. Who and what are we—we who have chosen Adventism? Who and what are you now that you have cast in your lot with this people?

What Is a Seventh-day Adventist?

Seventh-day Adventists are first and foremost Christians. They accept the gospel of Jesus Christ—the good news of Jesus' death on the cross to pay the price for sin. Adventists believe that Jesus rose from the dead as He had predicted, and that He offers forgiveness of sins and eternal life to all who humbly accept Him. They take the Bible as God's Word and the supreme authority in religious belief. They believe that Jesus will soon come again to end the reign of evil and save His people.

Seventh-day Adventism arose from a particular understanding of Bible prophecy that came to prominence in the mid-nineteenth century. Adventists felt called to leave the established Christian churches in order to prepare to meet the Lord, whom they believed would come in 1844. They now refer to this time as "the Great Disappointment." When Jesus did not come as expected on October 22 of that year, those who clung to their faith in prophecy studied further and discovered that they had been correct in identifying the date but wrong in the significance they assigned it. Jesus had indeed begun to vindicate His sanctuary, but it was in heaven, not on earth.

Adventism has not lost that sense of being "called out," or chosen. Elizabeth Platt, a Presbyterian minister, called Seventh-day Adventists "biblically covenanted people," meaning that they have a unique identity springing from the Bible. This has given the group a cohesiveness.

"When your youth leave the church, they know that they have left something special," a Dutch Reformed Christian told us—a little enviously, we thought. "When they are ready to settle down and return to God, they will return to

Adventism. Our young people don't have the same attitude toward the church." Indeed, surveys of former Adventists reveal that extremely few have left the Adventist Church because they rejected the doctrines. They leave because of differences with the people.

When people on the street are asked what they know about Adventists, usually they reply in terms of our distinctive marks—such as Sabbathkeeping or a vegetarian diet. But in fact, Seventh-day Adventists have more beliefs in common with other Protestants than differences. Even the Sabbath, probably our most distinctive belief, is held by several other small Protestant groups. Only our teaching of Jesus' ministry of the pre-Advent judgment's commencing in 1844 is truly unique. However, the Adventist configuration of doctrines—the total package of a logical, harmonious whole—also is unique.

Adventists believe in God as Trinity and Jesus as eternally divine, just like other evangelical Christians. But we do not accept the common Protestant belief in hell—that God consigns sinners to burn forever.

Many people who choose Adventism do so because of the sound biblical basis of the beliefs and the deeper understanding of God and His saving activity. Others are attracted to the church first by the earnest, loving commitment of the church members. Only later do they discover the beliefs from which the loving actions spring.

"I studied into many different religions," Lynn Bratcher says. "I met members of many different denominations. Nowhere did I find people more loving, caring, and forgiving than in the Adventist Church. I think it's because of the distinctive concept of a more caring, loving God."

Three years teaching public school opened Noelene's eyes to what it means to be Adventist. She had worked with some wonderful people there, one of whom was as fine a Christian as she'd ever met. But in the workplace, Adventists stand out, she thinks. They aren't perfect; they sometimes dispute among themselves. But they don't hold grudges for long. They know how to forgive because they worship a supremely loving and forgiving God.

Students of the Bible

Seventh-day Adventists are more than loving, caring Christians, however. They are students of the Bible. The church grew out of a deep searching of the Scriptures. For at least two generations Adventists depended upon careful Bible study to prove their beliefs and justify their right to existence. Today the benefits of their lifestyle speak for themselves, and attract people who, unfortunately, depend less on discovering truth from the Bible.

Seventh-day Adventists have 27 fundamental beliefs. Each is based on careful Bible study. Their content may be summarized as follows:

No. 1—The Holy Scriptures

Nos. 2-5—God: Father, Son, and Holy Spirit

Nos. 6-10—God's plan for our redemption (Creation, the Fall, Christ's incarnation and saving death, new life in Him)

Nos. 11-17—The church (its mission, unity, ordinances, and spiritual gifts)

Nos. 18-22—Christian Life (God's law, the Sabbath, stewardship, marriage and family)

Nos. 23-27—The last things (Christ's heavenly ministry and second coming, the millennium, and the new earth) (For a complete statement of these beliefs see the Appendix.)

Although the fundamental beliefs provide the doctrinal basis of Adventism, their wording leaves some leeway for individual interpretation. So Adventists may differ in their explanation of their beliefs according to their educational background, their basic philosophy of life, or how long they have been "in the way." This makes for considerable interest, even excitement, when they discuss beliefs publicly.

Every decade or two, it seems, debate about the cardinal

beliefs tends to heat up and passions flare. Those whose faith depends on a tight package of infallible beliefs fight to keep their package intact. But Adventism has no creed but the Bible, and the wording of the fundamental beliefs continues to be refined with the passing years.

Indeed, Ellen White, the writer who most influenced Adventist doctrine, clearly states that Christians are to continually dig for truth in the Scriptures. Truth will withstand the closest scrutiny, she said.

Following her example, Adventists have long upheld the Bible and the need for regular, personal Bible study. When individuals allow this concern for daily personal devotions to slip, the distinctive caring, loving quality of their Christian life tends to blur.

The Sabbath school grows out of the Adventist concern for study of the Bible. Designed to involve members in study, worship, and mission, the Sabbath school also provides an opportunity for laypeople to lead out in worship.

A typical Sabbath school begins at 9:15 a.m. Beautifully decorated rooms behind or beneath, sometimes above, the main sanctuary (meeting place) accommodate the children's and youth divisions of the Sabbath school. Dedicated leaders adapt the basic components of Sabbath school for the various age levels.

Music, prayer, stories from real-life experiences, Bible study, discussions, and witnessing are blended into a whole that, with some variation, follows a distinct pattern. Where churches are small enough, the large group breaks up into smaller units for the lesson study discussion. Anybody may be called upon to take part in the large group service, but usually people have at least a week to prepare.

Chances are that the first time you visit Sabbath school, the small group time could come as a shock, especially if the various groups all meet in the sanctuary. They begin quietly enough. But as the various teachers warm to their topics, the noise level rises. But usually so does the interest level. This unique feature sounds irreverent. However, it tends to make worship more meaningful because it allows people to discover how the Bible impacts on daily life.

Mission

A third feature of the Adventist identity is its sense of mission and worldview.

Seventh-day Adventists take the gospel commission seriously. They understand it to mean that all people everywhere have a right to hear the gospel with the distinctive Seventh-day Adventist understanding. So they see the world as their parish.

No other Protestant church has attempted so truly a global mission. Adventists have established churches in about 185 of the world's 213 nations listed by the United Nations. The sacrifice of members in developed nations, particularly North America, has helped to fund schools, churches, clinics, and hospitals and has staffed them with salaried missionaries.

Today these institutions are largely staffed by well-qualified national personnel, who aren't called missionaries unless they leave home and serve in an alien culture. So mission statistics show a marked decrease in the number of missionaries serving the church in the 1980s, not because Adventism is withering, but because nationals are taking over the work.

Older Adventists, in particular, love to hear and read about missions. Traditional Sabbath schools feature missions for at least 10 minutes each Sabbath morning. This sometimes surprises newcomers if they don't see the same interest displayed for reaching out to the local community.

Outreach at home is really the basis of the church's mission. While we talk about missions in terms of sending money overseas, when you get to the mission fields you discover that the gospel is spread there the same way it is at home—by laypeople reaching out into their communities.

Witnessing door-to-door was once an important part of

the Adventist identity in the United States. Adventists used to dream up excuses to knock at doors and get to know people. Once a year we tried to reach every home with an appeal for missions. People enjoyed our colorful brochures and gladly gave. We also took leaflets explaining our beliefs from door-to-door and invited people to public lectures.

But today people seem less ready to open their doors, and we have grown fearful of knocking. We prolong the discussions about mission and witnessing, and bring in the experts to demonstrate how to do it. But we need new believers to take us by the hand and say, "I just came from out there. People need what you have to give. It's not that bad. I'll knock and introduce you if you'll tell them what you know." We must reach out and share what we have, or we'll lose it.

Generosity

A discussion of our mission would not be complete without mentioning Adventist generosity. Seeing ourselves as stewards of the Lord's blessings helps us give what seems to others like large sums of money.

"Do you still give all that money to the church?" a non-Adventist relative asked recently. "Isn't it one tenth that you are expected to give? How do you do it?" I smiled. What would she say if she knew that many Adventists give a double tithe?

"It's all in your way of looking at it," I told her. "We don't look at it as 'all that money.' We take out the tithe first, and truly never miss it." How can we communicate the blessing that comes with entering into a covenant of systematic giving? In some mysterious way, the Lord honors His promise in Malachi 3:8-12 to pour out a blessing on those who take Him at His word.

Sociologists have documented the fact that Seventh-day Adventists tend to rise faster than average on the socioeconomic ladder, whichever culture they belong to. Adventists didn't know that would happen when they first advocated tithing, when they gave an average 3 percent of income to missions as well. We give now because it seems consistent with our understanding of the gospel and God's purpose for us.

To be fair, we must point out that stewardship is not as widely practiced in affluent societies as might be expected. Subsistence farmers in Africa and Asia often give a more faithful tithe than Americans. Even so, offerings still run much higher in Adventist churches than in other American denominations. About 50 percent return a faithful tithe.

Standards

A final aspect of the Adventist identity springs from our heightened awareness of God's love and sacrifice for us. Adventists respond to that love by trying to live a life worthy of our Saviour's name. So we set high standards of conduct that are truly a part of our identity.

Newcomers to Adventism discover that observance of these standards has created an Adventist subculture. We follow certain routines with regard to Sabbathkeeping. Friday, for instance, is usually a busy preparation day. We play special music Friday evenings and eat a special meal. Having 24 hours free from work has made us more family-oriented and also accounts for a disproportionate number of Adventists who are interested in nature and music.

What we eat and how we dress also have a particularly Adventist style. About half of all Adventists in the United States choose a vegetarian lifestyle. Almost all Adventists refrain from eating pork products. Studies have brought our natural diet to the attention of the American public. Many Americans have now modified their eating habits. They don't realize that Adventists provided the basis for many of the early studies on health and nutrition.

Adventists are inveterate label readers. We instinctively notice the calorie count and check for animal fat, particularly lard. Adventists feel genuinely sick at the thought of eating lard. That's why your Adventist friends were so quick to introduce health into their Bible studies. They love the way they eat; they think you'll love it too.

The same goes for dress. After being submerged in the Adventist subculture for a while, earrings, rings, and necklaces will begin to look positively heathen. We have to be reminded to keep our balance. In our eagerness to protect our children from worldliness, we go overboard. We let outward appearance threaten our balance. On this point we are at our most vulnerable.

Every once in a while someone stands up and preaches a sermon about getting back to the basics, "the blueprint," they call it. The departure from standards of dress and Sabbathkeeping do slip, and we truly need to be prodded to remember. The problem arises when we work on the outward signs of our apostasy instead of going back to our Bibles and renewing our relationship with God. After all, what we do is mere legalism without God's motivating love.

Continually harping about how to practice Adventism can be counterproductive. Jesus said much more about love than Sabbathkeeping and nothing at all about jewelry. This doesn't mean that we should give up our standards. But we should keep them in perspective. The secret of true Adventism is to hold fast the faith while at the same time loving and accepting those whose spiritual journey hasn't yet brought them to accept the same standards of lifestyle.

We can make an idol of almost anything. Take rings or earrings, for instance.

We give them up in the first place because we don't want them to be idols—to get in the way of complete surrender to God. But then we come to enjoy the elegance of simplicity. Rings and earrings come to look heathen to us. The no-rings concept often becomes our idol. So much so that one church refused to vote transfer of membership for a young woman because she wore a wedding ring. They wanted to keep their fellowship "pure." They allowed their love of simplicity to override Christian love and fellowship.

Nurturing Adventist Identity

The best way to nurture the Adventist identity is to live as a truly surrendered Adventist. We must daily study the Bible and ask God to point out the changes needed in our lives. Meddling in someone else's practice of Adventism spoils the culture and distorts the Adventist identity for others.

Another "must" for developing a Seventh-day Adventist identity is to continually question Adventism, discuss Adventism, and read about Adventism. We should never blindly copy what other Adventists do, but weigh ideas against biblical principles, remember that we must give account to God, not to church members.

Subscribing to Adventist papers helps us understand where Adventists are coming from and what they are discussing. We recommend studying the *Sabbath School Lesson Quarterly* each week and attending Sabbath school. There's no better place to strengthen your identity. We also recommend subscribing to and reading the *Adventist Review* and Adventist journals for the children *(Our Little Friend, Primary Treasure, Guide)* and youth *(Insight).*

Noelene and I often travel around the world. Everywhere we go, we notice certain people that we can clearly identify as Adventists, though their culture is quite different from ours. Often the people who stand out as loving, caring, responsible church members tell us, "We take the *Adventist Review.*" The church paper helps keep families in the church, keeps people aware of their church, and helps them grow.

By all means try to develop your Adventist identity. Feed the culture for your children. But don't put too much faith in lighting candles on Friday night or eating potato salad for Sabbath dinner. What you eat or wear or do is not nearly as important as keeping the love of Jesus burning in the heart.

10

Other Situations You May Face

You have made the most important choice of your life—you have chosen to be a Seventh-day Adventist Christian. The Lord wants you to experience His joy and peace day by day, as you grow in His knowledge and love. In the days ahead you'll face many situations. They often will challenge and put to the test your new identity as a Seventh-day Adventist. At home, on the job, at church—you'll find yourself asking questions, seeking for answers, reflecting on what it means to be an Adventist in the world. In effect, you'll be choosing again, reaffirming and confirming the choice you made for Adventism.

The Lord doesn't want Noelene or me or anyone else to tell you just how you should relate to any particular circumstance you may face. "Work out your *own* salvation," He advises (Philippians 2:12). But we can certainly learn from others. In this chapter we will tell you briefly about various Adventists we have known and how they dealt with some new situations. Even though your circumstances won't be exactly as theirs, their stories may help you.

Cathy and Ray

Cathy had been brought up a Roman Catholic. Her relatives were all Catholics, and the man she married, Ray, was also a Catholic. Cathy and Ray had children and were raising them as good Catholics.

But they found Adventism, and their life changed with dramatic suddenness. As they studied the Bible together, they became convinced that the Lord wanted them to keep holy the seventh day of the week, the Sabbath. Having learned that Jesus is our high priest in the heavenly sanctuary, they no longer felt the need for a human priesthood. Cathy and Ray began to think seriously about breaking with their family's Catholic tradition to join the Seventh-day Adventist Church.

Their relatives weren't at all pleased. As they discussed religion back and forth with Cathy and Ray, they brought up something that greatly troubled the young couple.

"Have you thought about what will happen to you when you die?" they queried. "No, we're not talking about whether you go up or down, but about where you'll be buried. As Catholics you have no problem—you can be buried in the consecrated ground the church has set aside. But if you leave the Catholic faith to join the Seventh-day Adventists, they'll not allow you to be buried there when you die."

Cathy and Ray were worried. This objection was something entirely new. To hear their relatives speak, Seventh-day Adventists didn't belong in the burial area reserved for Christians!

But they didn't abandon their quest. They brought up the matter to the Adventist pastor who had been leading them in study of the Scriptures.

"Yes," he said, "it's true that if you become Seventh-day Adventists you can't be buried in the Catholic cemetery. But that doesn't mean you'll have a problem with burial. All Protestants face the same situation. Seventh-day Adventists are buried in cemeteries set apart for Protestants."

He went on to explain what Adventists think about burial and the biblical teaching about death and resurrection. Nowhere in the Bible, he pointed out, do we find that God's people need to be interred in a particular plot of ground. There's no such thing as consecrated ground that will make a difference to a person's eternal destiny. What counts for eternity is how we live our life here and now. In fact, the Bible doesn't teach that we must be buried. Many Christians, some Adventists included, are cremated after their death.

The focus of the Bible's teaching about death, he explained, is in the doctrine of resurrection. This teaching shows us that God isn't dependent upon the molecules and atoms of our old body when He raises the dead. Resurrection means a new creation. At the second coming of Jesus, God breathes into wonderful new bodies and minds the personalities from our previous life.

Ray and Cathy felt relieved. They thought and prayed about the matter, studied the Bible passages concerning death and resurrection for themselves, and decided to go ahead. They would choose Adventism, even though they no longer could be buried in the Catholic cemetery.

Angela

Angela chose Adventism after she had married Joe. He didn't quite see the light; nevertheless, he respected Angela's beliefs. Often he would accompany her to church. For a while things seemed to be going fine: Angela noticed subtle changes in Joe that led her to hope that her prayers would be answered and soon he too would choose Adventism.

But a change came into her spiritual life. One Sabbath after church one of the members gave her some pamphlets to read. "Here, you ought to read these," the member said. "They'll tell you what's really happening in our church."

"What do you mean?" said Angela.

"Oh, the leaders of our people try to keep the truth from getting out. The General Conference is full of men who are concerned only about their own power and position. The Seventh-day Adventist Church has gone astray, and we've got to get back to the historic truths. I'm glad there are still a few people who are prepared to give the trumpet a certain sound. Read these pamphlets and you'll see what I mean."

Angela was confused. She had gladly joined the Seventh-day Adventist Church and rejoiced in her new experience. But could it be that she had not been told the whole truth?

She accepted the pamphlets and took them home to read. They made her even more troubled. The writer was surely correct, she thought, since he seemed to quote from Ellen White so much. But if he was right, then the Seventh-day Adventist Church was in a bad way. Its leaders had set out to take the church in the wrong direction. Most members had compromised the faith, and these leaders were either too lazy or too cowardly to rebuke them.

As Angela studied the pamphlets, she realized that the writer was challenging readers to make a separation within Adventism. He wasn't calling them to leave the church; rather, they should become part of an elite group that adhered to the historic teachings and practices of the church.

Earnest for the Lord, Angela found much in his words that appealed to her. She wanted to follow Jesus all the way. If He expected more of her than the pastor who studied with her had told her, then she would obey.

The pamphlet gave a mailing address, and she wrote away for more literature. She absorbed herself in it. The more she read, the more condemned she felt and the more sure she became that the great majority of members in the church were not walking in the Lord's light. But she wouldn't be like them; she would do everything that these writings suggested, no matter how hard they might be.

Meanwhile Joe noticed a change in Angela. Something had happened to her joyous, vibrant nature. She had become critical of the pastor, his sermons, the General Conference, and other members. She was suspicious. She was harder to live with, and she frequently found fault with him.

Joe lost all interest in attending church with her. He quit coming.

Then Angela's life took another turn. A new pastor came to the church. He was a good Bible student who could study the text in its original languages. Many of his sermons were more like Bible studies. Still seeking to follow God's will but increasingly disturbed and troubled, she decided she would discuss matters with him.

The pastor listened sympathetically. He appreciated her earnestness and zeal for the Lord. But he knew he faced a delicate task and prayed that the Holy Spirit would give him words that might reach Angela.

"The secret of Christianity is looking to Jesus, not to ourselves," he told her. He showed her from the Bible how the cross is at the heart of the plan of salvation, how it is to be the science and song of the redeemed throughout the ceaseless ages of eternity. He turned to Ellen White's writings and showed that our sufficiency before God can never be in our own works, but only in the righteousness of Jesus.

He pointed out that there are two errors against which we must guard. First, that by our own works we can commend ourselves to God. Nothing we can do or say, he explained, can add anything to the merits of Christ. Second, that the righteousness of Christ, which is reckoned to us by faith, leaves us unchanged. That righteousness, he pointed out, transforms us into the character of the lovely Jesus. He read to her the parable of the two debtors in Matthew 18:21-35. He showed her that the grace of God, which is His incredible generosity in forgiving us our sins, transforms us into merciful, forgiving, and loving beings.

But what about the church and its leaders, Angela wanted to know. Weren't they keeping the truth from the people? Weren't they leading the church astray?

The pastor listened. Again he turned first to the Bible and then to the writings of Ellen White. He showed how the church is the body of Christ, precious in His sight. It is the work of the evil one to accuse the leaders and to tear down the church, he said. Although the church is frail and defective, although its leaders make mistakes because they are human, Jesus still loves the church. It is His bride, the purchase of His blood. Have nothing to do with anyone or any writing that seeks to pull down the church, he advised.

Angela listened, intent, fascinated. And the pall that had hung over her spirit for months began to lift.

Angela found, in a new and precious way, the experience of Jesus and His saving righteousness. She learned to compare herself with Him, not with others. Rejoicing in His saving grace, she became less suspicious and judgmental.

And Joe noticed the difference in her. Once again he attends church with Angela.

Peter

I met Peter again recently when I went back to the little church that I first joined after I chose Adventism.

Peter is several years younger than I, and I had not seen him for a long while. I was glad to see him active in church affairs, serving as one of the elders. But his Sabbath school class, which Noelene and I attended, impressed us most.

In the midst of teaching the lesson, Peter suddenly paused. With deep emotion he said, "My wife and I stopped going to church for two years. But some dear people here loved us too much to let us go!"

I thought back over the years. That conference had been hit hard by doctrinal disputes. Many members had been upset by allegations concerning Ellen White—that she borrowed most of the material for her writings, that she could not have been the Lord's messenger to His people. Even some of the ministers in the conference had lost their way and had dropped out of the church.

These tumultuous spiritual times had rocked Peter and his wife. Although they had been brought up as Seventh-day Adventists, perhaps they had never had to think through the church's teachings themselves. Their faith had not been severely challenged before. And faced with questions they could not answer, listening to the doubts others were raising, Peter and his wife stopped attending church.

Whereas Angela had begun to fall prey to some unbalanced elements in the church, Peter and his wife had fallen into the slough of indifference. Fortunately, like Angela, they found their way back into full fellowship.

The instrument the Lord used to help Peter and his wife was people. People who did not give up on them. People who cared. People who kept in touch with them, letting them know they were missed. People who loved them too much to let them go.

Mohammed

Mohammed was a soldier in the Indian Army. Wounded in battle, he was sent to a hospital in Poona, in central India, to recuperate. Then facing discharge, he spent several months in a training school to learn a trade. Mohammed learned electrical wiring.

I was teaching at the time at Spicer Memorial College, the senior educational institution of the Southern Asia Division, located in Poona. Sabbath afternoons young men and women from the college fan out into the neighboring suburbs to conduct branch Sabbath schools for the children and to study the Bible with anyone who may be interested. Thus it came about that Mohammed met Manzoor, a ministerial student at Spicer.

Mohammed wasn't interested in studying the Bible, however. But Manzoor began to point out how many stories of the Old Testament are found in the Koran, the scriptures of Islam. As he read the stories of Abraham, Isaac, Ishmael, Jacob, and David, Mohammed was fascinated. He wanted to know more about the Christians' Bible.

After several weeks of study, Mohammed was close to becoming a Christian. The Lord was tugging at his heart, but he wasn't quite ready to make the break.

"Don't put off the day of decision," urged Manzoor.

"Life hangs by a slender thread!"

But Mohammed could not bring himself to choose Jesus. He completed his training and left Poona for a city in the north of India, many hundreds of miles away. We lost all contact with him.

One day we received a letter. "I want to be a Christian; I want to be baptized," wrote Mohammed. He told how he had begun to work in his trade of electrical wiring. One Saturday afternoon he and his companion were riding their bicycles on their way to a movie theater. Suddenly a bus swung into the curb, and Mohammed in horror saw his friend thrown to the pavement and under the wheel of the bus, killed outright.

Shaken, he returned home—and wrote the letter. "I remember your words, Manzoor," he said. "I remember how you told us that life hangs by a slender thread, that we must not put off the day of decision. That's why I want to become a Christian."

Because there was no Adventist pastor in the city, Mohammed decided he would come to Spicer Memorial College, enroll for a semester of schooling, and be baptized there. He gathered together his fees and told us the train on which he would arrive.

The train pulled in, but Mohammed was not on it. We wrote back to him but received no reply. We wrote again, but Mohammed seemed to have vanished.

Then several weeks later, out of the blue, we received a hastily written note from him. "I've had such trouble," he said. "The night before I was to leave to come to Spicer College, my uncle found out my plans. When I came home from work that evening, he locked the door, took down the rifle from the wall, pointed it at me, and said, 'If you become a Christian, you are a dead man!'

"While I slept, they took away my clothes. They took my money and my train ticket. When I woke up, I found myself a prisoner in my own home.

"They brought a Muslim priest to try to get me to change my thinking. He would come every Friday [the holy day for Muslims] and teach me from the Koran. But he didn't get anywhere, so they got another teacher—a high priest. After working with me for several weeks, he said to my uncle, 'I can't do anything with this fellow. Something has happened to his mind!'

"At last they let me go back to work. I'm writing this letter from work. What shall I do?"

We wrote back immediately, sending the letter to his workplace. "Mohammed, come to us at once. We'll send you a money order through the mail. When you receive it, get on a train and come to Poona."

And that is how Mohammed came to Spicer College. After further studies he was ready to follow his Lord in baptism. As I baptized him, I said to myself, "Here is a person who truly loves the Lord. Mohammed is no rice Christian!"

Mohammed stayed for a while at Spicer College. He eventually married an Adventist girl and left to work in electrical wiring.

When Mohammed chose Adventism, he lost all that he had and faced the threat of losing his very life! But he went forward, esteeming the reproach of Christ greater treasures than all the wealth of this world, than all the ties of family and friends.

Few if any of us will ever face a situation that compares with Mohammed's. But everyone who chooses Adventism will be tested. We will have to decide—again and again—if Jesus and His call are more important to us than anything else in this life.

I think they are. Jesus is wonderful! And so are His people—despite their faults.

Paul spoke for me when he said: "But whatever was to my profit I now consider loss for the sake of Christ. What is more, I consider everything a loss compared to the surpassing greatness of knowing Christ Jesus my Lord, for whose sake I have lost all things. I consider them rubbish, that I may gain Christ and be found in him, not having a righteousness of my own that comes from the law, but that which is through faith in Christ—the righteousness that comes from God and is by faith. I want to know Christ and the power of his resurrection and the fellowship of sharing in his sufferings, becoming like him in his death, and so, somehow, to attain to the resurrection from the dead" (Philippians 3:7-11, NIV).

APPENDIX

Fundamental Beliefs of Seventh-day Adventists

Seventh-day Adventists accept the Bible as their only creed and hold certain fundamental beliefs to be the teaching of the Holy Scriptures. These beliefs, as set forth here, constitute the church's understanding and expression of the teaching of Scripture. Revision of these statements may be expected at a General Conference session when the church is led by the Holy Spirit to a fuller understanding of Bible truth or finds better language in which to express the teachings of God's Holy Word.

1. The Holy Scriptures

The Holy Scriptures, Old and New Testaments, are the written Word of God, given by divine inspiration through holy men of God who spoke and wrote as they were moved by the Holy Spirit. In this Word, God has committed to man the knowledge necessary for salvation. The Holy Scriptures are the infallible revelation of His will. They are the standard of character, the test of experience, the authoritative revealer of doctrines, and the trustworthy record of God's acts in history. (2 Peter 1:20, 21; 2 Timothy 3:16, 17; Psalm 119:105; Proverbs 30:5, 6; Isaiah 8:20; John 17:17; 1 Thessalonians 2:13; Hebrews 4:12.)

2. The Trinity

There is one God: Father, Son, and Holy Spirit, a unity of three coeternal Persons. God is immortal, all-powerful, all-knowing, above all, and ever present. He is infinite and beyond human comprehension, yet known through His self-revelation. He is forever worthy of worship, adoration, and service by the whole creation. (Deuteronomy 6:4; Matthew 28:19; 2 Corinthians 13:14; Ephesians 4:4-6; 1 Peter 1:2; 1 Timothy 1:17; Revelation 14:7.)

3. The Father

God the eternal Father is the Creator, Source, Sustainer, and Sovereign of all creation. He is just and holy, merciful and gracious, slow to anger, and abounding in steadfast love and faithfulness. The qualities and powers exhibited in the Son and the Holy Spirit are also revelations of the Father. (Genesis 1:1; Revelation 4:11; 1 Corinthians 15:28; John 3:16; 1 John 4:8; 1 Timothy 1:17; Exodus 34:6, 7; John 14:9.)

4. The Son

God the eternal Son became incarnate in Jesus Christ. Through Him all things were created, the character of God is revealed, the salvation of humanity is accomplished, and the world is judged. Forever truly God, He became also truly man, Jesus the Christ. He was conceived of the Holy Spirit and born of the virgin Mary. He lived and experienced temptation as a human being, but perfectly exemplified the righteousness and love of God. By His miracles He manifested God's power and was attested as God's promised Messiah. He suffered and died voluntarily on the cross for our sins and in our place, was raised from the dead, and ascended to minister in the heavenly sanctuary in our behalf. He will come again in glory for the final deliverance of His people and the restoration of all things. (John 1:1-3, 14; Colossians 1:15-19; John 10:30; 14:9; Romans 6:23; 2 Corinthians 5:17-19; John 5:22; Luke 1:35; Philippians 2:5-11; Hebrews 2:9-18; 1 Corinthians 15:3, 4; Hebrews 8:1, 2; John 14:1-3.)

5. The Holy Spirit

God the eternal Spirit was active with the Father and the Son in Creation, Incarnation, and redemption. He inspired the writers of Scripture. He filled Christ's life with power. He draws and convicts human beings; and those who respond He renews and transforms into the image of God. Sent by the Father and the Son to be always with His children, He extends spiritual gifts to the church, empowers it to bear witness to Christ, and in harmony with the Scriptures leads it into all truth. (Genesis 1:1, 2; Luke 1:35; 4:18; Acts 10:38; 2 Peter 1:21; 2 Corinthians 3:18; Ephesians 4:11, 12; Acts 1:8; John 14:16-18, 26; 15:26, 27; 16:7-13.)

6. Creation

God is Creator of all things, and has revealed in Scripture the authentic account of His creative activity. In six days the Lord made "the heaven and the earth" and all living things upon the earth, and rested on the seventh day of that first week. Thus He established the Sabbath as a perpetual memorial of His completed creative work. The first man and woman were made in the image of God as the crowning work of Creation, given dominion over the world, and charged with responsibility to care for it. When the world was finished it was "very good," declaring the glory of God. (Genesis 1; 2; Exodus 20:8-11; Psalm 19:1-6; 33:6, 9; 104; Hebrews 11:3.)

7. The Nature of Man

Man and woman were made in the image of God with individuality, the power and freedom to think and to do. Though created free beings, each is an indivisible unity of body, mind, and spirit, dependent upon God for life and breath and all else. When our first parents disobeyed God, they denied their dependence upon Him and fell from their high position under God. The image of God in them was marred and they became subject to death. Their descendants share this fallen nature and its consequences. They are born with weaknesses and tendencies to evil. But God in Christ reconciled the world to Himself and by His Spirit restores in penitent mortals the image of their Maker. Created for the glory of God, they are called to love Him and one another, and to care for their environment. (Genesis 1:26-28; 2:7; Psalm 8:4-8; Acts 17:24-28; Genesis 3; Psalm 51:5; Romans 5:12-17; 2 Corinthians 5:19, 20; Psalm 51:10; 1 John 4:7, 8, 11, 20; Genesis 2:15.)

8. The Great Controversy

All humanity is now involved in a great controversy between Christ and Satan regarding the character of God, His law, and His sovereignty over the universe. This conflict originated in heaven when a created being, endowed with freedom of choice, in self-exaltation became Satan, God's adversary, and led into rebellion a portion of the angels. He introduced the spirit of rebellion into this world when he led Adam and Eve into sin. This human sin resulted in the distortion of the image of God in humanity, the disordering of the created world, and its eventual devastation at the time of the worldwide flood. Observed by the whole creation, this world became the arena of the universal conflict, out of which the God of love will ultimately be vindicated. To assist His people in this controversy, Christ sends the Holy Spirit and the loyal angels to guide, protect, and sustain them in the way of salvation. (Revelation 12:4-9; Isaiah 14:12-14; Ezekiel 28:12-18; Genesis 3; Romans 1:19-32; 5:12-21; 8:19-22; Genesis 6-8; 2 Peter 3:6; 1 Corinthians 4:9; Hebrews 1:14.)

9. The Life, Death, and Resurrection of Christ

In Christ's life of perfect obedience to God's will, His suffering, death, and resurrection, God provided the only means of atonement for human sin, so that those who by faith accept this atonement may have eternal life, and the whole creation may better understand the infinite and holy love of the Creator. This perfect atonement vindicates the righteousness of God's law and the graciousness of His character; for it both condemns our sin and provides for our forgiveness. The death of Christ is substitutionary and expiatory, reconciling and transforming. The resurrection of Christ proclaims God's triumph over the forces of evil, and for those who accept the atonement assures their final victory over sin and death. It declares the Lordship of Jesus Christ, before whom every knee in heaven and on earth will bow. (John 3:16; Isaiah 53; 1 Peter 2:21, 22; 1 Corinthians 15:3, 4, 20-22; 2 Corinthians 5:14, 15, 19-21; Romans 1:4; 3:25; 4:25; 8:3, 4; 1 John 2:2; 4:10; Colossians 2:15; Philippians 2:6-11.)

10. The Experience of Salvation

In infinite love and mercy God made Christ, who knew no sin, to be sin for us, so that in Him we might be made the righteousness of God. Led by the Holy Spirit we sense our need, acknowledge our sinfulness, repent of our transgressions, and exercise faith in Jesus as Lord and Christ, as Substitute and Example. This faith which receives salvation comes through the divine power of the Word and is the gift of God's grace. Through Christ we are justified, adopted as God's sons and daughters, and delivered from the lordship of sin. Through the Spirit we are born again and sanctified; the Spirit renews our minds, writes God's law of love in our hearts, and we are given the power to live a holy life. Abiding in Him we become partakers of the divine nature and have the assurance of salvation now and in the judgment. (2 Corinthians 5:17-21; John 3:16; Galatians 1:4; 4:4-7; Titus 3:3-7; John 16:8; Galatians 3:13, 14; 1 Peter 2:21, 22; Romans 10:17; Luke 17:5; Mark 9:23, 24; Ephesians 2:5-10; Romans 3:21-26; Colossians 1:13, 14; Romans 8:14-17; Galatians 3:26; John 3:3-8; 1 Peter 1:23; Romans 12:2;

Hebrews 8:7-12; Ezekiel 36:25-27; 2 Peter 1:3, 4; Romans 8:1-4; 5:6-10.)

11. The Church

The church is the community of believers who confess Jesus Christ as Lord and Saviour. In continuity with the people of God in Old Testament times, we are called out from the world; and we join together for worship, for fellowship, for instruction in the Word, for the celebration of the Lord's Supper, for service to all mankind, and for the worldwide proclamation of the gospel. The church derives its authority from Christ, who is the incarnate Word, and from the Scriptures, which are the written Word. The church is God's family; adopted by Him as children, its members live on the basis of the new covenant. The church is the body of Christ, a community of faith of which Christ Himself is the Head. The church is the bride for whom Christ died that He might sanctify and cleanse her. At His return in triumph, He will present her to Himself a glorious church, the faithful of all the ages, the purchase of His blood, not having spot or wrinkle, but holy and without blemish. (Genesis 12:3; Acts 7:38; Ephesians 4:11-15; 3:8-11; Matthew 28:19, 20; 16:13-20; 18:18; Ephesians 2:19-22; 1:22, 23; 5:23-27; Colossians 1:17, 18.)

12. The Remnant and Its Mission

The universal church is composed of all who truly believe in Christ, but in the last days, a time of widespread apostasy, a remnant has been called out to keep the commandments of God and the faith of Jesus. This remnant announces the arrival of the judgment hour, proclaims salvation through Christ, and heralds the approach of His second advent. This proclamation is symbolized by the three angels of Revelation 14; it coincides with the work of judgment in heaven and results in a work of repentance and reform on earth. Every believer is called to have a personal part in this worldwide witness. (Revelation 12:17; 14:6-12; 18:1-4; 2 Corinthians 5:10; Jude 3, 14; 1 Peter 1:16-19; 2 Peter 3:10-14; Revelation 21:1-14.)

13. Unity in the Body of Christ

The church is one body with many members, called from every nation, kindred, tongue, and people. In Christ we are a new creation; distinctions of race, culture, learning, and nationality, and differences between high and low, rich and poor, male and female, must not be divisive among us. We are all equal in Christ, who by one Spirit has bonded us into one fellowship with Him and with one another; we are to serve and be served without partiality or reservation. Through the revelation of Jesus Christ in the Scriptures we share the same faith and hope, and reach out in one witness to all. This unity has its source in the oneness of the triune God, who has adopted us as His children. (Romans 12:4, 5; 1 Corinthians 12:12-14; Matthew 28:19, 20; Psalm 133:1; 2 Corinthians 5:16, 17; Acts 17:26, 27; Galatians 3:27, 29; Colossians 3:10-15; Ephesians 4:14-16; 4:1-6; John 17:20-23.)

14. Baptism

By baptism we confess our faith in the death and resurrection of Jesus Christ, and testify of our death to sin and of our purpose to walk in newness of life. Thus we acknowledge Christ as Lord and Saviour, become His people, and are received as members by His church. Baptism is a symbol of our union with Christ, the forgiveness of our sins, and our reception of the Holy Spirit. It is by immersion in water and is contingent on an affirmation of faith in Jesus and evidence of repentance of sin. It follows instruction in the Holy Scriptures and acceptance of their teachings. (Romans 6:1-6; Colossians 2:12, 13; Acts 16:30-33; 22:16; 2:38; Matthew 28:19, 20.)

15. The Lord's Supper

The Lord's Supper is a participation in the emblems of the body and blood of Jesus as an expression of faith in Him, our Lord and Saviour. In this experience of communion Christ is present to meet and strengthen His people. As we partake, we joyfully proclaim the Lord's death until He comes again. Preparation for the Supper includes self-examination, repentance, and confession. The Master ordained the service of foot washing to signify renewed cleansing, to express a willingness to serve one another in Christlike humility, and to unite our hearts in love. The communion service is open to all believing Christians. (1 Corinthians 10:16, 17; 11:23-30; Matthew 26:17-30; Revelation 3:20; John 6:48-63; 13:1-17.)

16. Spiritual Gifts and Ministries

God bestows upon all members of His church in every age spiritual gifts which each member is to employ in loving ministry for the common good of the church and of humanity. Given by the agency of the Holy Spirit, who apportions to each member as He wills, the gifts provide all abilities and ministries needed by the church to fulfill its divinely ordained functions. According to the Scriptures, these gifts include such ministries as faith, healing, prophecy, proclamation, teaching, administration, reconciliation, compassion, and self-sacrificing service and charity for the help and encouragement of people. Some members are called of God and endowed by the Spirit for functions recognized by the church in pastoral, evangelistic, apostolic, and teaching ministries particularly needed to equip the members for service, to build up the church to spiritual maturity, and to foster unity of the faith and knowledge of God. When members employ these spiritual gifts as faithful stewards of God's varied grace, the church is protected from the destructive influence of false doctrine, grows with a growth that is from God, and is built up in faith and love. (Romans 12:4-8; 1 Corinthians 12:9-11,

27, 28; Ephesians 4:8, 11-16; Acts 6:1-7; 1 Timothy 2:1-3; 1 Peter 4:10, 11.)

17. The Gift of Prophecy

One of the gifts of the Holy Spirit is prophecy. This gift is an identifying mark of the remnant church and was manifested in the ministry of Ellen G. White. As the Lord's messenger, her writings are a continuing and authoritative source of truth which provide for the church comfort, guidance, instruction, and correction. They also make clear that the Bible is the standard by which all teaching and experience must be tested. (Joel 2:28, 29; Acts 2:14-21; Hebrews 1:1-3; Revelation 12:17; 19:10.)

18. The Law of God

The great principles of God's law are embodied in the Ten Commandments and exemplified in the life of Christ. They express God's love, will, and purposes concerning human conduct and relationships and are binding upon all people in every age. These precepts are the basis of God's covenant with His people and the standard in God's judgment. Through the agency of the Holy Spirit they point out sin and awaken a sense of need for a Saviour. Salvation is all of grace and not of works, but its fruitage is obedience to the commandments. This obedience develops Christian character and results in a sense of well-being. It is an evidence of our love for the Lord and our concern for our fellowmen. The obedience of faith demonstrates the power of Christ to transform lives, and therefore strengthens Christian witness. (Exodus 20:1-17; Psalm 40:7, 8; Matthew 22:36-40; Deuteronomy 28:1-14; Matthew 5:17-20; Hebrews 8:8-10; John 16:7-10; Ephesians 2:8-10; 1 John 5:3; Romans 8:3, 4; Psalm 19:7-14.)

19. The Sabbath

The beneficent Creator, after the six days of Creation,

rested on the seventh day and instituted the Sabbath for all people as a memorial of Creation. The fourth commandment of God's unchangeable law requires the observance of this seventh-day Sabbath as the day of rest, worship, and ministry in harmony with the teaching and practice of Jesus, the Lord of the Sabbath. The Sabbath is a day of delightful communion with God and one another. It is a symbol of our redemption in Christ, a sign of our sanctification, a token of our allegiance, and a foretaste of our eternal future in God's kingdom. The Sabbath is God's perpetual sign of His eternal covenant between Him and His people. Joyful observance of this holy time from evening to evening, sunset to sunset, is a celebration of God's creative and redemptive acts. (Genesis 2:1-3; Exodus 20:8-11; Luke 4:16; Isaiah 56:5; 6; 58:13, 14; Matthew 12:1-12; Exodus 31:13-17; Ezekiel 20:12, 20; Deuteronomy 5:12-15; Hebrews 4:1-11; Leviticus 23:32; Mark 1:32.)

20. Stewardship

We are God's stewards, entrusted by Him with time and opportunities, abilities and possessions, and the blessings of the earth and its resources. We are responsible to Him for their proper use. We acknowledge God's ownership by faithful service to Him and our fellow men, and by returning tithes and giving offerings for the proclamation of His gospel and the support and growth of His church. Stewardship is a privilege given to us by God for nurture in love and the victory over selfishness and covetousness. The steward rejoices in the blessings that come to others as a result of his faithfulness. (Genesis 1:26-28; 2:15; 1 Chronicles 29:14; Haggai 1:3-11; Malachi 3:8-12; 1 Corinthians 9:9-14; Matthew 23:23; 2 Corinthians 8:1-15; Romans 15:26, 27.)

21. Christian Behavior

We are called to be a godly people who think, feel, and act in harmony with the principles of heaven. For the Spirit to re-create in us the character of our Lord we involve ourselves only in those things which will produce Christlike purity, health, and joy in our lives. This means that our amusement and entertainment should meet the highest standards of Christian taste and beauty. While recognizing cultural differences, our dress is to be simple, modest, and neat, befitting those whose true beauty does not consist of outward adornment but in the imperishable ornament of a gentle and quiet spirit. It also means that because our bodies are the temples of the Holy Spirit, we are to care for them intelligently. Along with adequate exercise and rest, we are to adopt the most healthful diet possible and abstain from the unclean foods identified in the Scriptures. Since alcoholic beverages, tobacco, and the irresponsible use of drugs and narcotics are harmful to our bodies, we are to abstain from them as well. Instead, we are to engage in whatever brings our thoughts and bodies into the discipline of Christ, who desires our wholesomeness, joy, and goodness. (Romans 12:1, 2; 1 John 2:6; Ephesians 5:1-21; Philippians 4:8; 2 Corinthians 10:5; 6:14–7:1; 1 Peter 3:1-4; 1 Corinthians 6:19, 20; 10:31; Leviticus 11:1-47; 3 John 2.)

22. Marriage and the Family

Marriage was divinely established in Eden and affirmed by Jesus to be a lifelong union between a man and a woman in loving companionship. For the Christian a marriage commitment is to God as well as to the spouse, and should be entered into only between partners who share a common faith. Mutual love, honor, respect, and responsibility are the fabric of this relationship, which is to reflect the love, sanctity, closeness, and permanence of the relationship between Christ and His church. Regarding divorce, Jesus taught that the person who divorces a spouse, except for fornication, and marries another, commits adultery. Although some family relationships may fall short of the ideal, marriage partners who fully commit themselves to each other in Christ may achieve loving unity through the guidance of the Spirit and the nurture of the church. God blesses the family and intends that its members shall assist each other toward complete maturity. Parents are to bring up their children to love and obey the Lord. By their example and their words they are to teach them that Christ is a loving disciplinarian, ever tender and caring, who wants them to become members of His body, the family of God. Increasing family closeness is one of the earmarks of the final gospel message. (Genesis 2:18-25; Matthew 19:3-9; John 2:1-11; 2 Corinthians 6:14; Ephesians 5:21-33; Matthew 5:31, 32; Mark 10:11, 12; Luke 16:18; 1 Corinthians 7:10, 11; Exodus 20:12; Ephesians 6:1-4; Deuteronomy 6:5-9; Proverbs 22:6; Malachi 4:5, 6.)

23. Christ's Ministry in the Heavenly Sanctuary

There is a sanctuary in heaven, the true tabernacle which the Lord set up and not man. In it Christ ministers on our behalf, making available to believers the benefits of His atoning sacrifice offered once for all on the cross. He was inaugurated as our great High Priest and began His intercessory ministry at the time of His ascension. In 1844, at the end of the prophetic period of 2300 days, He entered the second and last phase of His atoning ministry. It is a work of investigative judgment which is part of the ultimate disposition of all sin, typified by the cleansing of the ancient Hebrew sanctuary on the Day of Atonement. In that typical service the sanctuary was cleansed with the blood of animal sacrifices, but the heavenly things are purified with the perfect sacrifice of the blood of Jesus. The investigative judgment reveals to heavenly intelligences who among the dead are asleep in Christ and therefore, in Him, are deemed worthy to have part in the first resurrection. It also makes manifest who among the living are abiding in Christ, keeping the commandments of God and the faith of Jesus, and in Him, therefore, are ready for translation into His everlasting kingdom. This judgment vindicates the justice of God in saving those who believe in Jesus. It declares that those who have remained loyal to God shall receive the kingdom. The completion of this ministry of Christ will mark the close of human probation before the Second Advent. (Hebrews 8:1-5; 4:14-16; 9:11-28; 10:19-22; 1:3; 2:16, 17; Daniel 7:9-27; 8:13, 14; 9:24-27; Numbers 14:34; Ezekiel 4:6; Leviticus 16; Revelation 14:6, 7; 20:12; 14:12; 22:12.)

24. The Second Coming of Christ

The second coming of Christ is the blessed hope of the church, the grand climax of the gospel. The Saviour's coming will be literal, personal, visible, and worldwide. When He returns, the righteous dead will be resurrected, and together with the righteous living will be glorified and taken to heaven, but the unrighteous will die. The almost complete fulfillment of most lines of prophecy, together with the present condition of the world, indicates that Christ's coming is imminent. The time of that event has not been revealed, and we are therefore exhorted to be ready at all times. (Titus 2:13; Hebrews 9:28; John 14:1-3; Acts 1:9-11; Matthew 24:14; Revelation 1:7; Matthew 24:43, 44; 1 Thessalonians 4:13-18; 1 Corinthians 15:51-54; 2 Thessalonians 1:7-10; 2:8; Revelation 14:14-20; 19:11-21; Matthew 24; Mark 13; Luke 21; 2 Timothy 3:1-5; 1 Thessalonians 5:1-6.)

25. Death and Resurrection

The wages of sin is death. But God, who alone is immortal, will grant eternal life to His redeemed. Until that day death is an unconscious state for all people. When Christ, who is our life, appears, the resurrected righteous and the living righteous will be glorified and caught up to meet their Lord. The second resurrection, the resurrection of the unrighteous, will take place a thousand years later. (Romans 6:23; 1 Timothy 6:15, 16; Ecclesiastes 9:5, 6; Psalm 146:3, 4; John 11:11-14; Colossians 3:4; 1 Corinthians 15:51-54;

1 Thessalonians 4:13-17; John 5:28, 29; Revelation 20: 1-10.)

26. The Millennium and the End of Sin

The millennium is the thousand-year reign of Christ with His saints in heaven between the first and second resurrections. During this time the wicked dead will be judged; the earth will be utterly desolate, without living human inhabitants, but occupied by Satan and his angels. At its close Christ with His saints and the Holy City will descend from heaven to earth. The unrighteous dead will then be resurrected, and with Satan and his angels will surround the city; but fire from God will consume them and cleanse the earth. The universe will thus be freed of sin and sinners forever. (Revelation 20; 1 Corinthians 6:2, 3; Jeremiah 4:23-26; Revelation 21:1-5; Mal. 4:1; Ezekiel 28:18, 19.)

27. The New Earth

On the new earth, in which righteousness dwells, God will provide an eternal home for the redeemed and a perfect environment for everlasting life, love, joy, and learning in His presence. For here God Himself will dwell with His people, and suffering and death will have passed away. The great controversy will be ended, and sin will be no more. All things, animate and inanimate, will declare that God is love; and He shall reign forever. Amen. (2 Peter 3:13; Isaiah 35; 65:17-25; Matthew 5:5; Revelation 21:1-7; 22:1-5; 11:15.)